Disney

IDEAS BOOK

Written by
Elizabeth Dowsett

Contents

See page 62

See page 66

See page 72

See page 22

See page 20

See page 32

See page 78

See page 102

See page 42

See page 110

See page 158

Activities

See page 116

See page 120

See page 122

See page 166

See page 188

Craft

See page 146

See page 150

See page 184

Find Your Favourites

Everybody has a favourite Disney or Disney•Pixar movie – and we have projects for more than 50 of the best! Whether you prefer princes and princesses or talking toys, wicked witches or feisty fairies, you can find them in the list of movie titles below.

Before You Begin

The key to creating Disney magic is preparation, so here is some important information to read before you start. You'll also find useful crafting tips and tricks to help everything run smoothly and ensure you get the best results.

Important note to parents and carers

The projects in this book may require adult help and supervision, depending on your child's age and ability. Always ensure that your child uses tools that are appropriate to their age, and offer help and supervision as necessary to keep them safe.

Safety first

All of the projects in this book should be approached with care, so make sure you read these safety tips first!

- Keep young children (under six years of age) and pets away from the crafting area.

- Don't allow any ingredients to come into contact with your eyes or mouth.

- Don't eat or drink while creating a project.

- Paint and food colouring can stain surfaces and clothing. If you want to protect your hands, you could wear gloves.

- Wash your hands and clean all equipment when you have finished a project.

- If you have any allergies (such as to eggs, acrylic paint or essential oils), avoid projects that utilise these ingredients, substitute if possible or protect yourself appropriately.

- Sharp objects, such as scissors, craft knives, needles or pins, should be handled with care. Ask an adult if you need help when cutting, pinning or stitching.

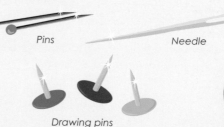

Pins   *Needle*

Drawing pins   *Scissors*

Acrylic paint   *Egg*   *Carrier oil*   *Food coloring*   *Essential oil*

Warning labels

Extra care or supervision is needed when you see these symbols:

Hot ovens, cooking equipment or irons are needed for this step. Ask an adult for help or supervision and take care when handling anything hot.

Ask an adult for help or supervision with this step.

Baking tray

How to use templates

This book includes templates on pages 190–199 to help you achieve the perfect shapes for the best end results in some of the more complicated projects. Follow the instructions at the back of the book.

Crafting essentials

Most of the supplies, ingredients and equipment used in this book are easy-to-find household products – you may have them in your desk drawer already! Everything else can be purchased online or at your local DIY, craft or stationery shop, department store or supermarket. Where we have specified a particular type of glue or paint, we have found that these materials give the best results. But this doesn't mean you have to use them if you have an alternate lying around or want to try something different.

Some key essentials are shown here:

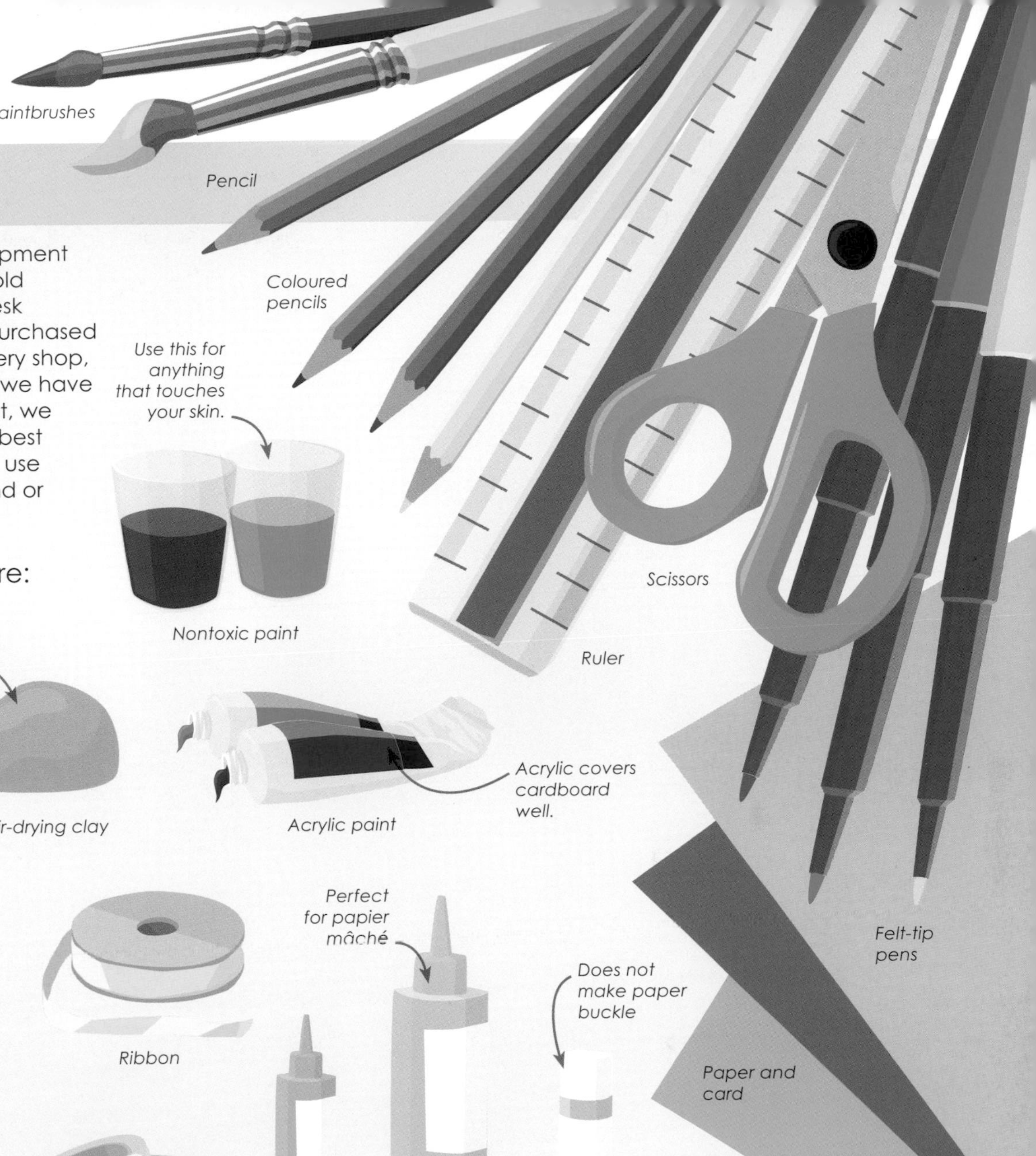

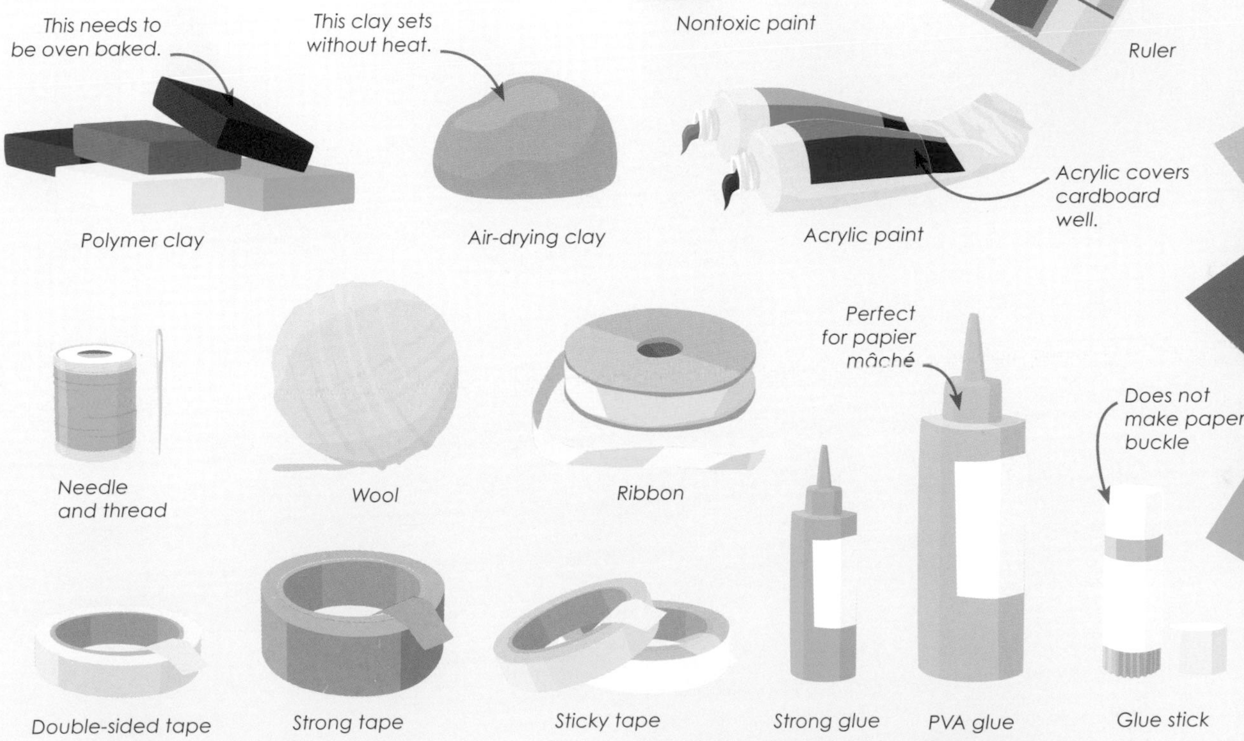

Paintbrushes

Pencil

Coloured pencils

Use this for anything that touches your skin.

Nontoxic paint

Scissors

Ruler

This needs to be oven baked.

This clay sets without heat.

Acrylic covers cardboard well.

Polymer clay

Air-drying clay

Acrylic paint

Felt-tip pens

Needle and thread

Wool

Ribbon

Perfect for papier mâché

Does not make paper buckle

Paper and card

Double-sided tape

Strong tape

Sticky tape

Strong glue

PVA glue

Glue stick

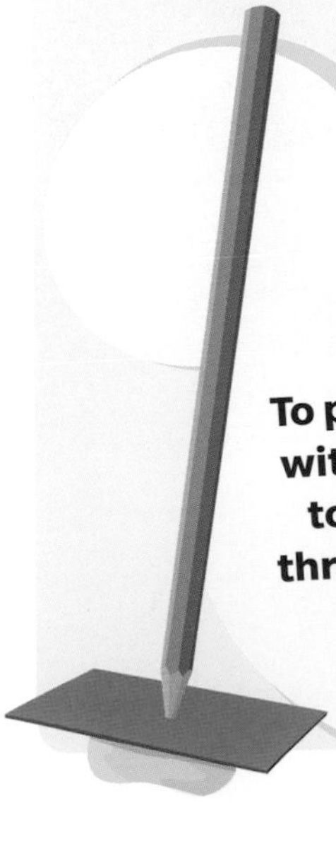

Egg boxes

Cardboard tube

Plastic bottle

TOP TIP
To punch a hole safely without a hole punch tool, press a pencil through paper or card into sticky tac.

GO GREEN!
We have tried to ensure our materials are recyclable – and you should, too! Use paper straws or raid your recycling for cardboard, bottles and other materials to keep your crafts eco-friendly.

Paper straw

MAKE BELIEVE

Flower Crown

Stand out from the crowd like Moana from the island of Motunui with your own leafy blossom crown. You might find it's the perfect accessory for a great adventure!

You will need:

- Elastic roughly 2½ cm (1 in) wide
- Scissors
- Needle
- Pencil
- Cotton thread
- Paper
- Sewing pins
- Felt
- Small beads

Measure your head

The crown is sewn onto an elastic band that should be snug around your head and easy to take on and off. Wrap the elastic around your head first to measure the size. Pull it slightly so it stretches a comfortable amount.

1 Add 2.5 cm (1 in) to the length and then cut the elastic.

2 Overlap the ends of the elastic by 2.5 cm (1 in), then sew them together using a simple running stitch, to make a headband.

TOP TIP
To speed up cutting out the leaves and flowers, layer several together and cut them all at once.

Cut out the felt

You'll need lots of leaves and petals to make your crown as full as Moana's. Cut out all these parts from felt. You could cut templates from paper and pin them to the felt to guide you.

1 Draw leaf and petal shapes on paper.

2 Cut out the paper shapes and pin them onto the felt.

3 Cut the felt shapes out. You will need: 28 dark-green leaves, 14 light-green leaves and seven pink flowers.

Assemble your flower crown

Once you've prepared the parts, all you need to do is sew them together. Then your crown is ready to wear!

1 Stack two dark-green leaves with a light-green one in the middle. Rotate each layer so the leaves fan out. Make seven of these stacks.

2 Sew each stack together with a few stitches in the centre of the leaves. Secure on the back with a knot.

3 Make seven more stacks of leaves. This time, top each stack with a pink flower and a bead.

4 Sew the new stacks together, taking the thread through the bead on top.

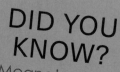

5 Stitch each stack onto the elastic. Alternate flower stacks with non-flower stacks. Sew them close together so the leaves overlap and stick out.

The leaf stacks nestle between the flower stacks to create a fuller feel.

DID YOU KNOW?

Moana's name means "Ocean" in many Polynesian languages. It fits her perfectly!

Cardboard Car Costumes

How does it feel to be a racing legend like Piston Cup champion Lightning McQueen? Step into his world with this cardboard-box-turned-race-car-costume to find out!

You will need:

- Cardboard box (big enough for you to fit in)
- Pencil
- Scissors
- Packing tape
- Acrylic paint
- Paintbrush
- Coloured paper
- Paper plates
- Split pin
- Wide ribbon
- Glue or double-sided tape

Shape your car

You'll need the four flaps from either the top or the bottom of your cardboard box to be intact. The other four can be cut off or folded inside the box. Cutting cardboard can be tricky, so ask an adult for help.

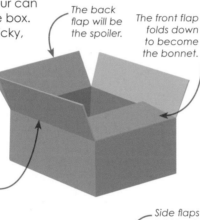

The back flap will be the spoiler.

The front flap folds down to become the bonnet.

1 Open all of the flaps on your box so they're standing upright.

2 Fold the front flap down.

The side flaps will be cut and shaped.

3 Cut along the join between the side flaps and the main box body, until you reach the point where the front flap is folded in. Do this for both side flaps.

4 Fold these two new flaps in so they meet in the middle of the box. Tape them together with packing tape to make the windscreen.

Side flaps fold in at right angles

Cut to here

5 For extra stability, tape the bottom of the windscreen to the edge of the front flap.

6 Cut a straight diagonal line on each side flap, from the top of the windscreen to the back flap.

7 Shape the back flap with scissors to make Lightning's spoiler.

8 Paint the whole body with red acrylic paint. Acrylic paint works best to cover cardboard, but you might need several coats.

Decorate your car

To wow spectators on the track you have to be fast, but it doesn't hurt to look sharp, too. Use paint and coloured paper to jazz up your car's bodywork.

Black paint works well for tyres, with bright red and yellow for hubcaps.

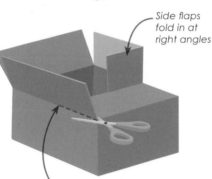

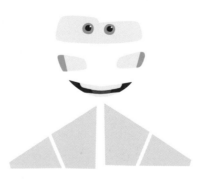

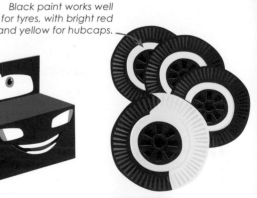

1 Once the red paint is dry, paint a "95" on both the long sides.

2 Cut shapes out of coloured paper for the side windows, eyes, headlights and mouth.

3 Stick the pieces of coloured paper to the car with glue or tape.

4 Paint four paper plates to look like wheels.

Card wing mirror

Wheels can really spin!

Cruz's body is shallower, with curved edges.

5 Attach each paper plate to the car with a split pin.

6 Ask an adult to help you measure the ribbon. You need to cut two pieces long enough to hold the car at a comfortable height, going over your shoulders. Crossing the ribbon at your back will hold the car more securely.

7 Use packing tape to attach the ribbon. You could paint over this tape to conceal it. Then you're ready to race!

TRY THIS!
Make Lightning's friend Cruz Ramirez in the same way, but paint her yellow and use different decorations.

13

Cardboard Candelabra

The charming candelabra Lumière brightens Belle's stay at the Beast's castle. Cheer up your room with your own Lumière. You just need cardboard, paint, glue – and voilà!

You will need:

- Pencil and black pen
- Cardboard
- Scissors
- Ruler
- Cardboard egg box
- 3 cardboard tubes
- Acrylic paint
- Paintbrush
- Glue
- 3 yellow pipe cleaners
- 2 googly eyes
- Black pen

Get prepared

Begin by cutting the cardboard shapes you need and painting them white or yellow.

2 Slice five cups from an egg box.

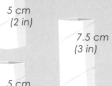

1 Cut three flames, one circular base and three round candle tops from cardboard.

3 flames

10 cm (4 in)

Candle base

3 candle tops

3 Carefully trim the cardboard tubes to the below lengths.

5 cm (2 in)

7.5 cm (3 in)

5 cm (2 in)

12 cm (5 in)

3 candle tubes for face and arms

Main body

Assemble Lumière

Once the paint is dry, work your own magic to bring the pieces together.

1 Cut a short slit in the bottom of all three flames. This creates two flaps.

2 Carefully make a slit the width of a flame in every candle top.

3 Now slot a flame into each candle top. Bend the flaps back and glue in place.

4 Once the candle tops are dry, glue them onto the candle tubes.

5 Using a pencil, make two tiny holes on opposite sides of the top of the tube.

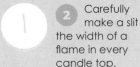

6 To build the stand, glue the yellow tube into an egg cup. Then glue the egg cup onto the circular base.

7 Twist three pipe cleaners together to make one thicker strand. This single length will make both of Lumière's arms.

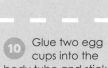

8 Push the arms through the two holes in the body until the pipe cleaners on each side are the same length.

9 Pierce a tiny hole in the bottoms of two egg cups with a pencil. Thread one onto each arm. Untwist the top of the pipe cleaners, spread the ends out and glue them down.

10 Glue two egg cups into the body tube and stick the longest candle tube on top.

Add detail to the candle flames with orange paint.

11 The two remaining tubes will be the candle hands. Glue them into the cups on each arm.

12 Stick on two googly eyes and use a black pen to complete Lumière's friendly face.

These pipe-cleaner arms can be bent to animate Lumière.

DID YOU KNOW?
Lumière is in fact a dashing Frenchman under a spell. He is the Prince's most-trusted servant.

CINDERELLA
Rags-to-Riches Apron

You may not have a fairy godmother, but with a flip of this double-sided apron you can be transformed from rags to riches in an instant. Just make sure to switch it back before midnight!

You will need:

- Iron
- Scissors
- Needle
- Cotton thread (white and blue)
- White, brown and light-blue fabric each 30 x 42 cm (11 x 17 in)
- 2 pieces of silky blue fabric 42 x 59 cm (16½ x 23¾ in)
- 3 strips of tulle 50 x 15 cm (20 x 6 in), plus extra for ties
- Blue ribbon 1 m (40 in) long
- Iron-on adhesive

Start with the rags

Cinderella wears a brown-and-white apron when she's doing her chores. It is very ragged from lots of use!

1 Ask an adult to iron your fabric to make sure it's crease-free.

2 Tear a rip in the white fabric, to make the apron look worn out.

3 Place the white fabric on top of the brown fabric.

Fold the top edge of the white fabric to stop it fraying.

4 Using the needle and white thread, stitch the two pieces of fabric together along the top edge and for 2 cm (¾ in) at the top of each side.

Making the ball gown

The ball gown side of the apron has a blue skirt parted to reveal a fluffy layer of tulle, with a light-blue base underneath.

1 Thread the needle with blue thread.

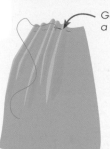

Gathering creates a ruched effect.

2 Starting from the edge, thread the needle at wide intervals through one of the pieces of silky blue fabric.

3 Pull the thread to gather the top of the fabric.

4 Secure the thread with a few stitches on top of each other, so it doesn't come undone.

5 Repeat with the second piece of silky blue fabric.

6 To make the tulle layer, start by threading the needle with white thread.

7 Gather the tops of the three strips of tulle, as you did with the blue fabric in steps 2 to 3.

Each strip of tulle is ruched.

8 Sew the three tulle strips onto the light-blue fabric.

Bring everything together

Once you have the two sides to your apron, you need to join them together and add ribbon so you can wear it.

1 Stitch the top of the two silky fabric pieces over the tulle, along the top of the light-blue base.

2 Stitch the top of the brown-and-white side to the top of the light-blue one.

3 Ask an adult to bond the ribbon on top of the ball gown side using iron-on adhesive.

4 Bond the bottom of the brown layer to the light-blue base.

5 Cut two small strips of tulle.

Wear your apron this way round to bake and switch it around to welcome your friends!

TOP TIP
You could strengthen your fabric by ironing hemming tape at the edges.

Ruched overskirt is bunched up to look fuller.

6 Gather the silky, blue fabric and tie each one with a tulle ribbon.

7 Fold the silky fabric under and secure to the base layer with a single stitch through the back of the tulle ribbon.

You can add more tulle to make your ball gown even fluffier!

17

Felt Animal Masks

When he was a young cub, Simba loved dreaming of when he would be king of the whole savannah. Now you can rule any party with this simple mask made from felt! Impress all your friends with your animal antics.

You will need:

- Tracing paper
- Pencil
- Paper
- Pins
- Coloured felt
- Scissors
- Double-sided tape
- Ribbon
- Thin cardboard
- Permanent black marker or fabric pen

Make a face

Layer up pieces of coloured felt to create Simba's head, including the mane he makes for himself out of red leaves. You can use the same technique to make other characters, such as Rafiki.

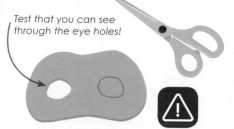

Test that you can see through the eye holes!

1 Using the templates on pages 190–191, copy the shapes onto paper and cut them out.

2 Pin each shape to the right-coloured felt and carefully cut them out.

3 Place the large face piece against your face to make sure that the eye holes line up with your eyes. Ask an adult to cut out the holes.

Smaller hair piece should go on top of the larger hair piece.

4 Line up the eye pieces around the eye holes and attach with double-sided tape. Below the eyes, layer and stick the muzzle and nose pieces.

5 On the top of the face, layer and stick on the orange and yellow hair pieces.

6 Turn the mask over and tape the ears to the back, so they stick out from behind the face.

7 Attach the mane behind everything else.

Get ready to roar

Adding cardboard will make your mask stronger. Backing it with felt will make it more comfortable against your face.

The ribbons will tie together behind your head to hold up the mask.

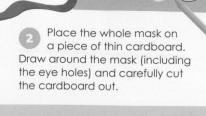

1 Cut two pieces of ribbon long enough for you to tie them behind your head. Tape one to each side of the mask, just above where your ears will be.

2 Place the whole mask on a piece of thin cardboard. Draw around the mask (including the eye holes) and carefully cut the cardboard out.

When he's imagining being grown up, Simba creates a mane from red leaves.

Male mandrills such as Rafiki have bright-red noses.

Mask

Cardboard support

Felt back

The ends of the ribbon will be secured within the layers.

3 Repeat step 2 with a piece of felt.

4 Tape the felt to the cardboard and tape that to the mask.

5 With a permanent black marker or fabric pen, add eyebrows, eye details, nostrils and ear details. Now you're ready to be king of the pride!

DID YOU KNOW?

"Simba" is the Swahili word for "lion".

Miguel's Guitar

Miguel longs to be a musician more than anything else. His disapproving family won't let him get a guitar, so he makes his own – and you can, too. Will yours be as treasured as Miguel's?

Make your guitar
Strumming this guitar makes real sounds, thanks to elastic bands stretched around a hidden plastic box.

You will need:

- Thick corrugated cardboard
- Pencil
- Scissors
- Paint and paintbrush
- Plastic container, such as a food container
- Elastic bands
- White card
- Ruler
- Strong tape
- Double-sided tape
- Black pen
- Silver card
- Glue
- Wooden skewer
- 2 black pipe cleaners
- 6 black buttons

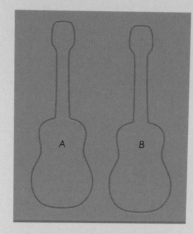

1 Carefully cut two guitar shapes from corrugated cardboard: pieces A and B. You may need an adult's help for the smaller details.

2 Cut a hole in the middle of piece A.

DID YOU KNOW?
When Miguel's homemade guitar is smashed, he acquires the guitar of the legendary singer Ernesto de la Cruz. To Miguel's astonishment, it transports him to the Land of the Dead.

3 Paint a black circle on piece B that is a little larger than the hole on shape A.

4 Wrap three elastic bands lengthways around the plastic container.

Container sits over the black circle.

5 Attach the container to the base of piece B with double-sided tape.

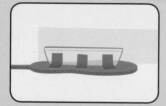

6 Cut out two long strips of white card. Make sure the width is bigger than the height of the plastic container.

7 Make tabs by cutting slits in the card strips all the way along each side, and fold them over.

Don't cut too far in. Leave enough to cover the height of the container.

8 Stick the strips all around the base of the guitar, using double-sided tape to secure the tabs to the base, following the shape of the guitar.

Decorate your guitar

Miguel makes his guitar with passion rather than professional skill, so it has a rough-and-ready look.

Skull face with teeth

Six teeth

1. Paint the top and bottom of the guitar white.

2. Draw or paint on decorations.

For frets, draw lines spaced 2 cm (1 in) apart.

Yellow squares surround the border.

Decorative, swirling pattern

You can strum or pluck the "strings".

3. Cut a cardboard comb shape roughly the width of the hole. Paint it black and glue it below the hole.

4. Cut out a piece of silver card, draw nail details with a black pen and glue it on the guitar.

5. Cut three elastic bands open. These will become decorative strings.

6. With the skewer, make holes in the skull's teeth, about 1 cm (½ in) apart. Thread one end of each of the bands through each hole.

7. Tuck the other end of the bands through the centre circle and tape to the underside. Line them up with the food container elastic bands.

8. Connect the top of the guitar to the tabs with double-sided tape.

The thicker the elastic band, the deeper the sound it will make.

Add tuning pegs

For an even more authentic-looking guitar, add these simple tuning pegs.

1. Using a skewer, make three holes on each side of the top of the guitar.

2. Cut two black pipe cleaners into six pieces.

3. Attach a black button to the end of each pipe cleaner.

4. Thread each pipe cleaner into a hole, with the button sticking out.

Selfie Props

Pose as your favourite Disney hero – or villain – with a collection of fun selfie props. Create some fabulous accessories, gather your friends and make your own photo booth. Lights, camera, action!

Make your props

These selfie props are made from coloured paper stuck onto card to make them more rigid. Each one has a wooden dowel to hold onto.

You will need:

- White paper
- Pencil
- Coloured paper
- Card
- Scissors
- Glue
- Wooden dowels
- Sticky tape

1 Choose which characters' accessories you want to make – or design your own.

2 Sketch your picture to work out the shapes you need.

3 Draw each shape on the correct coloured paper.

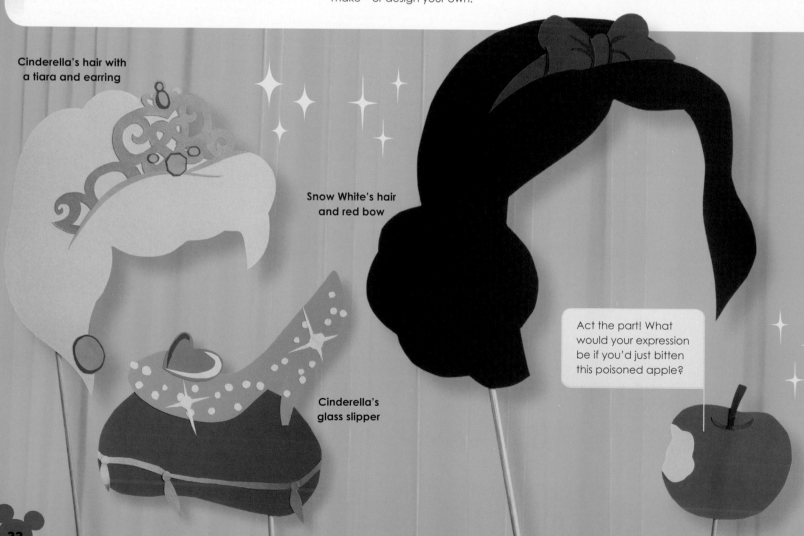

Cinderella's hair with a tiara and earring

Snow White's hair and red bow

Cinderella's glass slipper

Act the part! What would your expression be if you'd just bitten this poisoned apple?

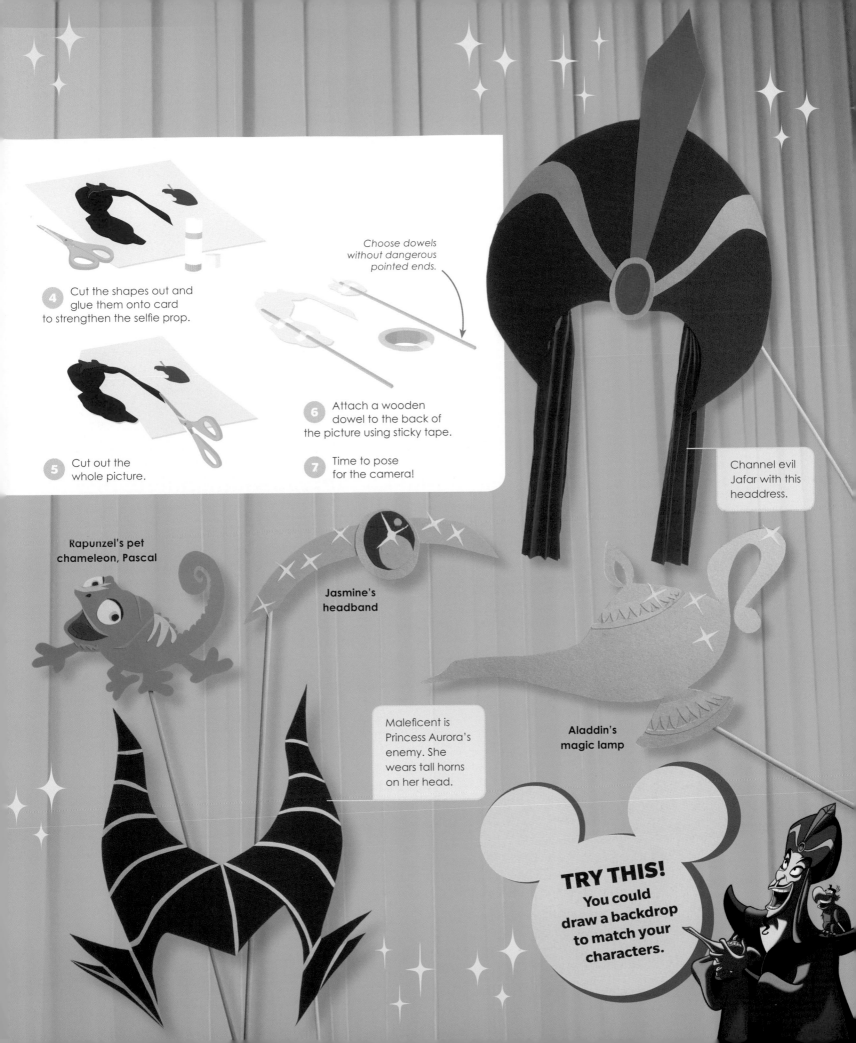

4 Cut the shapes out and glue them onto card to strengthen the selfie prop.

5 Cut out the whole picture.

Choose dowels without dangerous pointed ends.

6 Attach a wooden dowel to the back of the picture using sticky tape.

7 Time to pose for the camera!

Channel evil Jafar with this headdress.

Rapunzel's pet chameleon, Pascal

Jasmine's headband

Aladdin's magic lamp

Maleficent is Princess Aurora's enemy. She wears tall horns on her head.

TRY THIS!
You could draw a backdrop to match your characters.

Be in the frame

Dress up your selfie prop photographs with a frame fit for a prince or princess – or even a villain! Made from metallic card or paper, an ornate frame is a perfect part of any royal photo booth.

Salt-Dough Necklace

Pocahontas's father gives her a special necklace when she is due to marry. In fact, it marks the start of a very different life for her. Craft one like it to wear for adventures of your own.

Make the dough

This simple mixture is easy to mould into any shape. It goes completely hard when it's cooked.

1. Pre-heat the oven to 100°C (225°F).

You will need:

- 100 g (3½ oz) plain flour
- 100 g (3½ oz) salt
- 65 ml (2¼ oz) water
- Mixing bowl
- Blunt knife
- Drinking straws
- Baking tray
- Oven
- Acrylic paint
- Paintbrush
- Needle and cord
- Scissors

2. Mix the flour, salt and water, and knead the dough with your hands until it forms a smooth mixture.

Shape and bake

Pocahontas's necklace is made from four wide beads and a diamond-shaped bead with a decorative piece on top.

1. Cut the dough into five pieces. Shape four of them into wide beads.

2. Using a straw, make a hole in each wide piece. Keep the straws in place for now.

The wide bead should be shaped like a rounded rectangle.

3. With the fifth piece of dough, make a diamond shape with a long, thin strand to wrap around the cord.

4. Add a smaller, flat diamond shape of dough on the pendant for decoration.

Squeeze these pieces together, or use water, to make them stick.

5. Bend the pendant's long strand around a straw, making a loop.

6. Remove straws and place all of the shapes on a baking tray.

7. Bake the dough in the oven for 2 hours.

TOP TIP
Salt dough is great for crafting, but not for eating!

Thread the necklace

Once your beads have cooled, you can paint them "all the colours of the wind"… but turquoise would match Pocahontas's necklace!

1. Paint thin layers of acrylic paint on each bead until you have a strong, solid colour.

Try pale grey for the pendant.

2. Wait until each layer has dried before adding the next.

3. Measure the cord so the necklace will fit over your head. Cut the cord to the right length, allowing an extra 10 cm (4 in) for tying.

4. Thread the cord through the beads. You could use a thick needle to help.

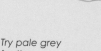

5. Tie the cord in a knot.

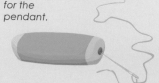

Paint paler details at the ends of the wide pieces.

You could also make a necklace like strong Powhatan warrior Kocoum's.

DID YOU KNOW?
Pocahontas's necklace used to belong to her mother.

Elsa's Sparkly Cape

Elsa uses her magical powers to create ice and snow, and to give herself a sparkly new look with a frosted, glittery gown. Fashion yourself a flowing cape to channel your inner Elsa.

You will need:

- White sheer fabric, at least 1½ times your height
- Pale-blue sheer fabric, at least 1½ times your height
- Fabric pen
- Scissors
- Thread

- Needle
- Wide ribbon
- Pencil
- Paper
- Pins
- Double-sided tape
- Fabric glitter, gems, and fabric glue (optional)

Make the cape

The main part of Elsa's cape is just two large pieces of fabric, sewn together at the top.

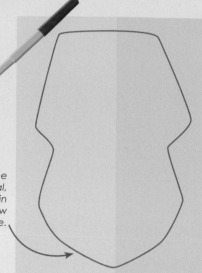

1 Draw the shape shown onto both fabrics. The shape on the blue fabric should be a little smaller than the shape on the white fabric.

2 Cut out both shapes.

To make the cape symmetrical, fold the fabric in half, then draw half the shape.

3 Place the smaller shape on top of the larger one so that they line up at the top.

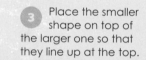

4 Sew the top edges of the fabric together. ⚠️

TOP TIP
When you're drawing on and cutting out the long pieces of fabric, lay them flat on the floor and ask someone to hold them still for you.

Add arm loops

A busy, active princess can't risk her cape falling off. This one is held up by two simple loops around the top of the arms.

1 Cut two pieces of ribbon. You could use strips of the sheer cape fabric.

2 Make a loop with each one and tie with a knot, leaving the ends trailing.

Make sure that this loop will fit around your upper arm.

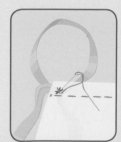

3 ⚠️ Sew these ribbon loops onto the top two corners of the cape.

4 Tie the trailing ends of the ribbons into neat bows and adjust to fit.

Add icy details

Sheer fabric glistens a little already, but you can add snowy decorations and more sparkle for a full *Frozen* effect.

1 Draw snowflake shapes on paper and cut them out to make templates.

2 Pin the snowflakes to leftover pieces of fabric and cut them out.

3 Attach the snowflakes to the cape with double-sided tape or fabric glue.

4 You could add fabric glitter and gems to your cape using fabric glue, but be careful not to stick the cape to the floor!

Elsa's gown has an off-the-shoulder style.

DID YOU KNOW?

Queen Elsa's frosty magical power can be beautiful and fun, but when it's out of control it brings winter to all of Arendelle. With the help of her sister, Anna, Elsa learns to control her powers.

Snowflake detail

Playing-Card Costumes

Dress up as a walking, talking playing card with this no-sew costume. These cards work for the Queen of Hearts, but you don't have to – you could form your own pack of cards!

Plan your cards right

These instructions show how to make the Five of Hearts, but you can adapt them for any number or suit. Ask an adult to iron your pillowcase to remove any creases before you start.

You will need:

- Paper
- Pencil
- Scissors
- An old white pillowcase
- Red or black felt
- Fabric glue or double-sided tape
- Cardboard tube
- Glue stick
- Paint (optional)

1 Draw a heart roughly 15 cm (6 in) wide on paper and cut it out. This will be your template.

2 Use the heart template to cut out five felt hearts.

The ace card has one single suit symbol.

For higher-number cards, you may need to trim your template to fit.

Five of Hearts

Four of Clubs

Ten of Diamonds

Ace of Hearts

Three of Spades

3 Cut another paper heart template, smaller than the original. Use this heart template to cut out two more felt hearts. These will sit under the numbers.

4 Draw and cut out a paper "5". Use this as a template to cut out two felt numbers.

5 Lay the pillowcase down with the open end nearest to you. Arrange all the felt pieces on the pillowcase.

6 Stick each shape down with fabric glue or double-sided tape. If you want the back of the pillowcase to be decorated, too, repeat steps 2 to 6 on the other side.

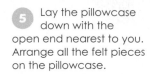

Make sure you ask permission before you cut or stick any pillowcases!

You could mark the size of your arms and neck in pencil first, to make sure the holes will be wide enough.

7 Ask an adult to cut out holes in the costume for your head and arms.

TRY THIS!
If your pillowcase is too long for you, you could trim it to make it shorter. You could also decorate a spare, plain t-shirt in the same way.

Make your sceptre
The card soldiers each carry sceptres of their suit. These ornamental staffs are simply made from rolled paper, cardboard tubes and felt.

1 Start by rolling a piece of red paper from one corner and secure it with glue or tape when you have made a cone.

2 Paint a cardboard tube red for a handle. Once dry, attach the cone to the cardboard tube with glue or double-sided tape.

Instead of using a cardboard tube, you could roll up a piece of card to make the handle.

3 Cut out two felt hearts using the larger template and stick them together, leaving a small opening at the bottom.

4 Slot the heart on top of the sceptre and secure it with glue or double-sided tape.

DID YOU KNOW?
A standard pack of playing cards has 54 cards: 13 in each of the four suits (hearts, diamonds, spades, and clubs) and two jokers.

Pirate Hook

Peter Pan is Captain Hook's sworn enemy. Thanks to Peter, the pirate captain lost his hand to a crocodile! Ever since, he has worn a steel hook. Make your own hook and join his crew!

You will need:

- Cardboard
- Pencil
- Glue
- Aluminium foil
- Paper cup
- Craft knife
- Scissors
- Sticky tape
- Lacy paper doilies
- Red felt
- Double-sided tape

Tease the doilies outwards to give Hook's shirt sleeves a full look.

Crimson frock coat

DID YOU KNOW?

The crocodile that ate Hook's hand follows him wherever he sails. He's always hoping for another taste!

Make the hook

This hook has a long handle for your hand to hold inside the paper cup. This stops the hook falling off your arm – even when you wave it around in battle!

1 Draw a hook shape with a long handle on cardboard and cut it out.

2 Wrap and glue strips of foil around the hook until it's fully covered.

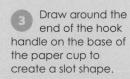

3 Draw around the end of the hook handle on the base of the paper cup to create a slot shape.

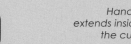

4 Ask an adult to cut the slot out of the cup with a craft knife.

5 Check that the hook fits into the slot.

Handle extends inside the cup.

Bring it all together

The paper cup is hidden by clothing that looks like Captain Hook's crimson frock coat.

1 Fold two lacy doilies into quarters.

2 Cut the corner off each doily.

3 Unfold the doilies and insert the ends through the hole around the hook.

4 Gather the paper around the hook and tape in place for a full, frilly look.

5 Cut a shape out of red felt that is a little narrower at the top than at the bottom. Make sure the top is wide enough to wrap around the cup.

This side should be roughly as long as your forearm.

6 Apply double-sided tape to seal the sleeve edges together.

7 Arrange the ruffles to hide the top of the cup.

Animal-Feet Stilts

In Mowgli's jungle, Shere Khan the tiger stalks, Bagheera the panther pads and Colonel Hathi the elephant stomps. Make these stilts and follow in these animals' mighty footsteps.

Make your feet

Plastic flowerpots can be decorated to look like any animal's feet and then used as stilts.

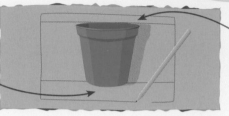

The base of the flowerpot will be the top of the stilt.

Leave extra material at the top of the flowerpot.

You will need:

- Two sturdy plastic flowerpots
- Animal-print fabric
- Pencil
- Scissors
- Double-sided tape or fabric glue
- White card
- Thick cord

TRY THIS! Make sure the pots hold your weight. You might need to double up and use two pots inside each other.

1 Roll your flowerpot over the fabric and mark out enough to wrap all the way around the pot.

2 Mark out an extra 2 cm (¾ in) at the top and enough to cover half of the flat base of the pot.

3 Measure and mark out the same amount of fabric for the other flowerpot. Cut out both pieces of fabric.

4 Stick the fabric around the flowerpots using double-sided tape or fabric glue. Leave the extra strips at the top and bottom unstuck.

5 Cut slits in the fabric that is sticking out both ends of the pot. Fold the base-side slits over and stick them to the flat base.

6 Fold the open-side slits over and stick them to the inside rim.

7 Cut out eight strips of fabric 10 cm (4 in) long and 3 cm (1½ in) wide for the toes. Roll them up lengthways and secure them with tape.

8 Cut eight equilateral triangles from white card, with each about 2.5 cm (1 in) wide.

9 Fold two corners down on each triangle and tape them down to make a diamond shape.

10 Tape one paper claw to each toe, then tape four toes to each pot.

Turn your feet into stilts

Flowerpots come with holes already made for threading your handles through, so they are perfect for stilts!

1 Ask an adult to pierce the fabric on top of the pot to free up two of the holes in the plastic pot.

2 Carefully stand on the pots to measure a length of cord for each foot.

3 Tie a knot in one end of the cord. Thread it through a hole from the inside of the flowerpot, then back through the second hole. Tie a knot in that end, too. Repeat for the other foot.

Elephant feet

To make elephant feet, follow the same steps as above, but use grey crepe paper instead of felt and create some elephant toenails out of paper shaped into curves.

Pull the cord taut to keep your balance while you walk.

Wrinkle the grey crepe paper to make it look like elephant hide.

If you don't have tiger-print fabric, you could use orange fabric and stick on your own black stripes.

Shark Cap

Everyone will see you coming with a shark fin on top of your head! Make an entrance wherever you go with this cap inspired by Bruce the great white shark.

Get prepared

All the shapes are cut from craft foam. Allow a little extra for flaps that will be folded over and stuck down.

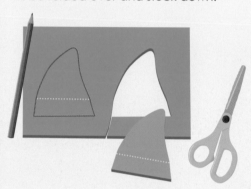

1 Draw two identical fin pieces on blue foam. Add a 1.5 cm (½ in) tab at the bottom of each, and cut them out. Check their size against your cap.

2 Draw two eyes and seven teeth on white foam and cut them out.

3 Draw pupils on the eyes with the black pen.

Bring it all together

Once you've prepared all the pieces, it's just a case of attaching them to the cap.

1 Glue the two fin pieces together except for the tab at the bottom. Fold these two flaps out at right angles to the fin.

Snip lines in the flaps to help them stick to the cap.

2 Glue the flaps down the centre of the top of the hat.

3 Fold the top of each tooth over to make a flap. Glue the flaps to the inside of the cap's brim.

4 Glue the eyes to the front of the cap. Leave everything to dry completely.

TOP TIP
If you don't have craft foam, you could cover pieces of card with coloured felt.

Primary dorsal fin

DID YOU KNOW?

As a shark on a fish-free diet, Bruce tries to befriend Dory and Marlin rather than eat them.

You only need to make seven of Bruce's 202 teeth!

Cupcake-Case Lei

Lilo gives Stitch a traditional lei as a symbol of their friendship. Lei are often given as gifts or worn at celebrations in Hawaii. Transport your friends to a tropical paradise with these flower garlands.

Flower power
Cutting out all the petals may seem like a big job, but you can cut a few at once, so it won't take long.

1 Stack a few cupcake cases together.

2 Fold the pile in half, then in half again.

The shape you cut will be repeated four times on your case.

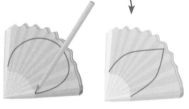

3 Draw on your design. You could do a rounded design for a petal or a pointed one for leaves.

4 Carefully cut out your design, leaving the centre intact.

5 Unfold the paper to reveal a symmetrical pattern.

Bring it together
Once you've gathered your petals and leaves, it's time to thread them into a garland. Check that it fits over your head first!

1 Measure thread so it's the right length for a garland, plus 10 cm (4 in) for tying.

3 To hold the petals in place, you can tie knots in the thread after every few cases.

2 Thread the needle and push it through the centre of a case. Pull it all the way through.

4 Add more cases. You can keep them facing the same way or alternate them inwards and outwards.

5 Tie the thread in a knot or bow, and it's ready to wear!

TRY THIS!
Patterned cupcake cases would give really different looks to your lei!

Alternating the way the petals are threaded will give your lei a fuller, floral look.

You can add green cases to look like leaves.

DID YOU KNOW?
Mischievous Stitch is an alien. He was created by a scientist on another planet.

Buzz Lightyear's Wings

Buzz is devastated to find out he's only a toy, but he soon discovers that you don't need to be a real Space Ranger to go on exciting expeditions. Make your own space wings and get ready to head to infinity and beyond!

You will need:

- Thick corrugated cardboard
- Scissors
- Pencil
- Ruler
- White paper
- Sticky tape
- Coloured paper or card
- Glue stick
- Double-sided tape
- Wide ribbon

Make your wings

To get off to a flying start, prepare the three pieces of thick cardboard that will form your wings.

⚠️ *Cutting thick cardboard may require adult supervision.*

1 Carefully cut out two rectangles of thick corrugated cardboard for the wings. Each should measure the same as the length from the middle of your back to the end of your outstretched arm.

2 Draw a diagonal line with a pencil and ruler along one edge of each wing to make them slanted. Cut along the lines.

3 Cover the top halves of the wings with white paper using tape, the way you would wrap a present.

4 Wrap the bottom halves of the wings with purple paper.

Cut the corners at a slight angle from halfway up on each side.

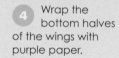

5 Cut out a smaller cardboard rectangle, a bit taller than your wings, and a bit narrower than your back.

6 Wrap this smaller piece of cardboard with white paper.

7 Stick a wide strip of silver paper across the bottom.

8 Tape the two wings together, joining them at their tallest edge.

9 Stick the back panel on top of the wings with double-sided tape.

Decorate your wings

The wings and back panel are decorated with coloured paper or card shapes for a bright, bold finish.

Wrap any excess over the edge of the wing.

There are lots of controls on Buzz's suit. You could copy his – which make him say funny catchphrases – or invent your own.

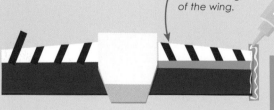

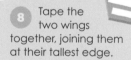

1 Cut out the shapes you need for decoration, as shown, or make your own.

2 Glue four red strips at an angle, evenly spaced, on each wing. Trim so they do not cover the purple paper.

3 Glue a long green strip along each wing, covering the joins between the purple, white and red paper.

4 Glue a short green strip around each end of the wings, sticking the overhang together.

5 Glue all the colourful control-panel shapes on the back panel.

Red, green, white, purple and silver are essential colours for replicating Buzz's spacesuit.

DID YOU KNOW?
Buzz Lightyear is a modern Space Ranger toy, working with Star Command to protect Sector 12 from Evil Emperor Zurg.

Red lights sit on a metal utility belt.

Buzz Lightyear's wings fold up into the back panel.

The ribbons should be long enough to tie comfortably around your arm.

TOP TIP
If you don't have cardboard big enough for the wings, you can tape smaller pieces together.

6 Ask an adult to hold the wings against you and work out the best place to attach the ribbon straps.

7 Cut and tape the ribbon in place to make arm loops. Now you're space-ready!

Felt Finger Puppets

Christopher Robin has many fun adventures with the animals in the Hundred-Acre Wood. Now you can, too, with these adorable finger puppets. Bring the characters to life with coloured felt and then put on a show.

You will need:

- Tracing paper
- Pencil
- Scissors
- Pins
- Coloured felt
- PVA glue or double-sided tape
- Black felt-tip pen

Make felt puppets

All the finger puppets shown use the same basic shape for the body. You can then customise the colours and add on any shapes you like.

1 Copy the templates on pages 192–193 onto tracing paper.

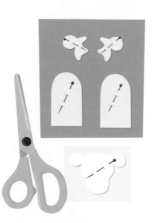

2 Cut out the tracing paper and pin the shapes onto felt.

Orange body (front)

Orange body (back)

Pale-yellow head

Peach tummy

Two orange ear pieces

Red mouth

Pink nose

3 Cut out the felt shapes.

4 Place the front and back body pieces together and check that your finger fits inside, allowing for the areas that will be stuck down.

The stitching on Eeyore's head is drawn with pen.

Tigger

Pooh

5 Stick the two pieces of felt together using glue or tape. Just stick around the edges, but not along the flat bottom edge.

DID YOU KNOW?

Winnie the Pooh and his friends were based on toys owned by a real boy named Christopher Robin, born in 1920. His father, A. A. Milne, wrote the original stories.

6 Arrange the tummy, head pieces, nose, mouth and stripes on top of the body. Stick them down with glue or double-sided tape when you are happy with their positions.

7 Draw on the eyes and stripes with a black felt-tip pen.

TOP TIP

On page 192–193, you'll find templates for all five of the characters. You can make them using the same steps.

Pooh's smile is a simple curved piece of red felt.

Piglet

Rabbit

Eeyore

Fairy Garden

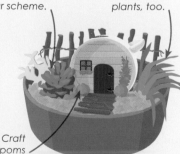

There's no place like home for Tinker Bell and the other Never Fairies, who live in the cosy nooks and crannies of Pixie Hollow. What can you find to make an enchanting garden fit for a fairy?

You will need:

- An old teacup or teapot
- Pencil
- Cardboard
- Thin card
- Scissors or craft knife
- Ice-lolly sticks
- PVA glue
- Felt-tip pens
- Sticky tac or sticky tape
- Moss
- Sequins
- Air-dry or polymer clay
- Acrylic paint
- Paintbrush
- Flowerpot or container
- Sand or soil
- Twigs
- String
- Pebbles or gravel
- Pine cones, leaves, sprigs, pebbles, shells, buttons, craft pom-poms etc. (optional)

Prepare your fairy house

Tinker Bell lives in a converted teapot, but you can make a fairy garden with an old teacup. Make sure that you have permission before you start!

1 Draw around the rim of your cup on a piece of cardboard. Use this to cut out a slightly smaller circle that will fit snugly in your cup.

The circle should fit just inside the cup.

2 Glue ice-lolly sticks across the circle.

3 Ask an adult to trim the sticks with a craft knife to remake the circle.

4 Draw a door and a window on card with felt-tip pens. Cut them out and glue them to your circle.

Glue your features to the lolly-stick side.

5 Secure the ice-lolly stick circle inside the cup using sticky tac or sticky tape.

6 Glue moss under the window and climbing up the wall. You could add sequin "flowers" with glue to make it look like a window box.

 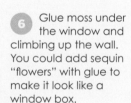 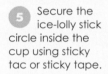

Bring it all together

The fairies in Neverland build and decorate their houses with whatever they can find. You can do the same, adding items you have on hand.

Make sure your cup sits securely and doesn't wobble.

1 Half fill a large flowerpot with sand or soil, and position your cup, slightly submerged in the sand.

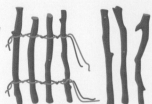

2 Make a fence by tying twigs together with string. Place the fence in the sand, around the edge of the flowerpot.

You could paint the pine cones to suit your colour scheme.

You could use real plants, too.

Craft pom-poms

3 Arrange twigs, pebbles or gravel for a path leading to the door.

4 Complete your fairy garden with pieces of moss, pine cones and any other finishing touches.

Make some mushrooms

Nothing says fairy-tale garden like red-and-white spotty mushrooms. Mould and add these fun fungi to your scene.

1. For each mushroom, divide a small ball of clay into two pieces, one larger than the other. Mould into mushroom shapes.

2. Leave the pieces to dry or bake them in the oven, following the package instructions. If baked, leave them to cool.

   Larger dome piece for top

   Smaller column shape for stem

3. Paint the stems white and the tops red with white spots. Glue the pieces together when dry.

If using real plants, position your fairy garden in an appropriate location.

Fence gives fairies some privacy.

DID YOU KNOW?

The fairy kingdom of Pixie Hollow in Neverland is home to hundreds of teeny-tiny fairies, including Tinker Bell.

Felt Ears

Creatures of all shapes and sizes live in Zootropolis. They have tall ears, small ears or even floppy ears. Dress up like furry crime-fighters Nick and Judy with these simple ears.

You will need:

- Child-size headband
- Felt
- Scissors
- PVA glue
- Wool or string
- Thin cardboard
- Felt-tip pens

Prepare the headbands

It doesn't matter whether you are making Nick's fox ears, Judy's bunny ears or the ears of another character – they all start with the same method.

Fold a thin strip of felt around the headband.

1 Cover the headband with felt in the colour of your chosen character, and attach with PVA glue. For Judy, use grey felt and for Nick, brown felt.

2 Wrap wool or string around the headband to hold the felt in place. Leave it to dry overnight.

3 Once the glue is dry, remove the wool or string.

Make Judy's ears

These tall rabbit ears have cardboard inside the felt layers so that they stand up straight.

1 Cut out all the felt and cardboard pieces.

2 cardboard support pieces

2 outer-ear felt pieces with tabs

2 middle-ear felt pieces   2 Inner-ear felt pieces

2 Glue the cardboard support to the centre of each grey felt outer ear.

The cardboard support should be slightly smaller than the white middle-ear piece.

3 Glue the white felt pieces onto the cardboard so that the supports are fully covered.

4 Stick the pink felt pieces onto the middle of each ear.

5 Wrap the tab of each ear up and over your precovered headband and glue in place.

6 Fold in the sides of grey felt and glue them down so they overlap at the front.

7 Shade the top of each ear with a dark-grey felt-tip pen.

Make Nick's ears

These foxy ears are made from diamond shapes folded over to become triangles.

1 Cut out all the felt and cardboard pieces.

2 cardboard support pieces

2 inner-ear felt pieces

2 outer-ear diamond felt pieces

2 ear-tip felt pieces

2 Glue the cardboard support triangles inside the top half of each brown felt diamond, as in step 2 for Judy.

3 Glue the black felt triangles on top of the cardboard of each ear, so that they extend above the brown felt.

4 Position your brown felt-covered headband across the middle of the two diamonds.

5 Wrap the bottom half of each diamond up and over the headband and glue in place.

Leave some of the black tip visible.

6 Glue the cream triangles on the front of each ear.

DID YOU KNOW?

Judy's tall ears help her to hear the clicking noises parking meters make. This skill makes her the fastest parking attendant Zootopia has ever seen!

Make sure the headband fits comfortably.

Pumpkin Carriage

Here's a craft to make you feel just like Cinderella's fairy godmother. Believe it or not, you can transform a pumpkin into a carriage that's fit for a royal ball. With a bit of luck, your carriage might even last beyond midnight!

Prepare your pumpkin

Find the most evenly shaped pumpkin that you can. Before you start, wash off any dirt.

You will need:

- Carving pumpkin with its stem still on
- Pumpkin carving tools or a knife and spoon
- Acrylic paint
- Paintbrush
- Pencil

- Scraps of pink satin
- Scissors
- Two straight pins
- Glue
- Wide, wired ribbon
- Small, clear jar (optional)

1 Ask an adult to cut a hole in the bottom of the pumpkin. Scoop out all of the insides.

If you can't find pearlescent blue paint, mix blue, white and metallic silver.

2 Ask an adult to help you carve a semicircular window.

3 Paint the pumpkin with pearlescent light-blue paint. You'll need two or three coats.

4 Leave it to dry completely.

5 Paint the stem metallic gold.

Bring it all together

Once your pumpkin is dry, it's ready for a magical transformation into a fairy-tale coach.

1 With a pencil, draw an oval-shaped door and a "C" for Cinderella in a crest.

2 Paint gold around the edge of the window and over your pencil lines.

3 Cut a rectangle of pink satin that will fit in your window.

4 Pin or glue the satin inside the pumpkin, and arrange it to look like curtains.

You could add glitter to the paint to make it more magical.

TOP TIP
To give your carriage a magical glow, you could put a small battery-operated light inside.

Curl the back wheel more tightly so it looks fuller than the front wheel.

5 Take a long piece of wired ribbon and wind each end into a tight curl. Repeat with a second piece of wired ribbon.

6 Rest the pumpkin on top of the ribbons. You can raise the pumpkin higher by using a jar as a stand.

7 Cut a crown shape from a wide piece of ribbon. Wrap the crown around the stem and glue it in place.

8 Cut thin strips of ribbon, wind them in tight curls, then glue them around the crown.

GAMES

THE PRINCESS AND THE FROG
Kiss the Frog

Tiana never thought she would want to kiss a frog. However, Prince Naveen, in frog form, changes her mind. Try out this froggy twist on a classic party game.

TOP TIP
Either leave all the lips on the frog until the end or write the player's initials in their place.

You will need:

- A large poster-sized piece of paper
- White card
- Felt-tip pens or paint
- Sticky tac
- Blindfold

Prince Naveen is a human who has been turned into a frog with bad magic!

1. Draw or print out a large picture of a frog.

2. Draw pairs of lips on the card, colour them different shades, and cut them out. You need at least one pair for each player.

3. Put your frog on the wall with sticky tac, roughly at eye level to the players.

4. Add some sticky tac to each of the lips and give one to each player.

HOW TO PLAY:

Players take turns being blindfolded and spun around three times. Then they stick their lips on the frog picture, as close to the mouth as possible. When everyone has had a turn, the winner is whoever's lips are nearest to the centre of the frog's mouth.

ALICE IN WONDERLAND
Flamingo Croquet

The Queen of Hearts plays croquet using flamingos and hedgehogs. With this mini version, you don't need live animals or large Royal Palace gardens to play. Let the games begin!

You will need:

- Tracing paper
- Pencil
- Pink card
- Scissors
- Chopsticks (one for each flamingo)
- Sticky tape
- Googly eyes (one for each flamingo)
- Glue
- Pipe cleaners
- Table-tennis ball
- Paint (optional)

Make your mallet
You can use the template to help you make your flamingo mallet.

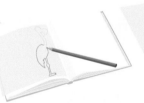

1 Trace the flamingo from the template on page 190 onto tracing paper.

2 Copy the flamingo shape onto pink card and cut out one for each player.

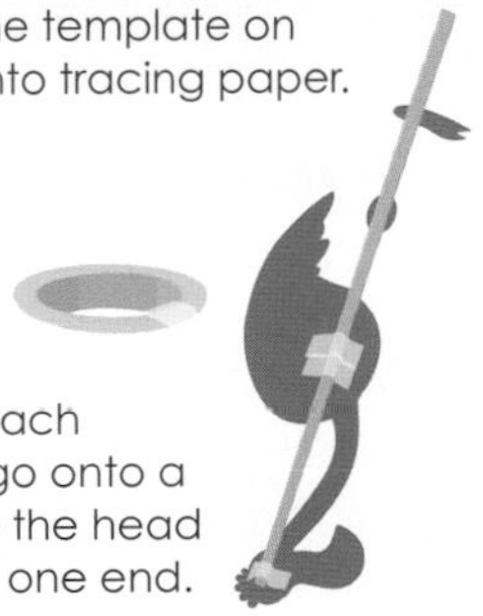

3 Tape each flamingo onto a chopstick so the head lines up with one end.

4 Stick a googly eye onto each flamingo.

Create the course
Pipe cleaners form perfect hoops for your mini course. Six would make a fun game!

1 Bend pipe cleaners into arches for each hoop.

2 Twist the ends of each hoop to make flat stands.

Spread out your hoops to make a tricky course.

TRY THIS!
You could decorate the table-tennis ball to look like a hedgehog!

HOW TO PLAY:

The first player tries to hit the ball through the first hoop. If they succeed, they move on to the next hoop. If they don't, then it's the next player's turn. The winner is the first person to finish the whole course.

Seven Dwarfs Skittles

Snow White's friends are in a playful mood – so they make the perfect skittles! See if you can knock them down with a red poisoned apple in this fun bowling game.

You will need:

- 7 cardboard tubes
- Scissors
- Sticky tape
- Small freezer bags
- Uncooked rice
- Paint and paintbrush
- Coloured felt
- Craft glue
- Gold card
- Felt-tip pens
- Cotton thread
- Tennis ball

Prepare your Dwarf

A cardboard tube weighted down with rice makes each Dwarf's skittle body.

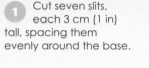

1 Cut seven slits, each 3 cm (1 in) tall, spacing them evenly around the base.

2 Fold the cut pieces into the middle.

3 Use tape to stick each piece down.

4 Check that your tube can stand up and adjust it if necessary.

5 Paint the top 5 cm (2 in) pale pink for the Dwarf's face.

6 Half fill a freezer bag with rice to weigh down the skittle.

Dress your Dwarf

Cut felt pieces in different colours to decorate your Dwarfs.

Belt

Arms

Hat

Coat

Feet

Hands

Beard Nose

1 Wrap the coat piece around the tube and glue the overlap at the back.

2 Add the beard to the front.

3 Stick a hand on both ends of the arm piece.

4 Glue the arm piece on, wrapping it around the back of the tube.

5 Glue the belt on top of the coat.

6 Cut buckles from gold card and stick them onto the belts.

7 Stick two feet at the bottom.

Make the base as flat as possible to help the Dwarf to balance.

8 Put the bag of rice inside the tube.

9 Glue the rectangular hat piece around the top.

10 Gather the material to seal the hat and fasten with thread.

11 Glue on the round nose piece.

12 Draw on a distinctive face. Try to capture the personality of the Dwarf you are creating!

Poisoned apple

A red apple, made from a tennis ball, will knock down your Dwarfs.

Leaf

Leaf

Stalk

1 Paint a tennis ball red.

2 Glue on felt leaves and a stalk.

HOW TO PLAY:

Line up the Dwarfs and take turns rolling the poisoned-apple ball towards them, standing them up again after each roll. The person who knocks over the most skittles wins!

DID YOU KNOW?

Apple dumplings and gooseberry pie are the Dwarfs' favourite foods.

Sleepy doesn't mind being knocked down. He's always ready for a snooze!

Which Sidekick Are You?

Every hero needs a sidekick to help them succeed on their adventures. A sidekick needs to help their hero – whether this means cheering them up, planning a mission, keeping them in check or simply being a best friend. What kind of sidekick are you?

Are you good at making people feel better?

Yes

No

Do you try to find the good in people?

Yes

Would you help your friend even if it puts you in danger?

No

Yes

Yes

No

Do you prefer telling jokes to playing pranks?

No

No

Yes

Do you always do as you're told?

Yes

Yes

No

START!

Do you love adventure more than anything else?

Yes

Are you helpful?

No

Are you super-confident?

Yes →

No →

No ↓

Do you sometimes do things you know are wrong?

Yes →

No →

Would you join your friend on an adventure – no matter what it was?

Yes →

TIMOTHY Q. MOUSE
Just like Dumbo's sidekick, you know your own strengths and you help your friends find theirs. Cheerful and encouraging, your friends wouldn't reach their true potential without you.

JIMINY CRICKET
You are working hard to be a good person and you kindly share your advice, like Pinocchio's cricket companion does. You are full of jokes – ready to make learning lots of fun!

MUSHU
You are as ambitious as Mulan's tiny dragon pal and you want your best friend to be the best, too. Sometimes things don't work out as planned, but you will get your friend there in the end!

TINKER BELL
You can be a little bit mischievous sometimes. But you will do anything to help your friends because you are endlessly loyal, like Peter Pan's fairy friend.

ABU
You are a true partner-in-crime, like Aladdin's pet monkey – there through the good and the bad. You are always ready for adventure and will never let your best friend down.

Echolocation

Dory's friend Bailey the beluga whale uses echolocation to help find his way around. Humans can't echolocate, but you can have a whale of a time with this game that uses your ears to find things.

You will need:

- A large space clear of obstacles and tripping hazards
- Blindfold (optional)

To the rescue

When Dory is lost in a maze of pipes, Bailey finds that his echolocation skills can help her, even from a distance. He guides her to safety from his tank.

HOW TO PLAY:

1. One person is the seeker. They close their eyes or are blindfolded. The aim of the game is for them to find another player by listening.

2. The seeker claps once and then all the other players must clap back.

3. Using this sound, along with any other noises made by the players like breathing or moving around, the seeker must try to locate them and gently tap them.

4. The seeker can clap up to five times. If they still haven't found anyone, the round is over.

5. As soon as someone is found, they become the seeker and a new round starts.

DID YOU KNOW?

Some whales use echolocation to hunt and find their way around. By emitting sounds that bounce off objects back to them, they can tell where those objects are.

TRANSFER 3181

Musical Flying Carpets

The Magic Carpet is Aladdin's friend. It helps Aladdin to win Jasmine's heart by flying the couple all around the world and towards the stars. See if your carpet can win you a prize in this party game.

Design your carpets

You could make carpets in advance, or each person could make their own as an activity before playing the game.

1 Decorate your piece of paper with pens or paint.

2 Cut short, thin strips all the way along the two shorter edges to make a fringe.

You will need:

- Paper (large enough to sit on)
- Scissors
- Pens or paint
- Music and music player
- Someone to play music

Arabian carpets like Aladdin's often have symmetrical patterns.

HOW TO PLAY:

For the first practice round, you need the same number of carpets as players. Lay the carpets on the floor in a circle. When the music is played, all the players move or dance around them. When the music stops, everyone must sit on a carpet (one person per carpet). In each round, one carpet is removed. Whoever doesn't have a carpet to sit on when the music stops is out. The winner is the last person still in the game.

DID YOU KNOW?

The Magic Carpet is really clever and loves to play chess. Poor Genie loses almost every time.

Feeling adventurous?

You can make the game more challenging by adding a task players must complete before they sit down. For example, players could do five star jumps or walk backwards while moving around the carpets.

Dogcatcher

The Tramp tries to protect his friends from the dogcatcher. He doesn't want to see them locked up! See if you can rescue your friends from capture with a new take on the game of tag.

You will need:

- Tape or chalk

DID YOU KNOW?

The Tramp affectionately calls Lady "Pidge". It's short for "Pigeon".

HOW TO PLAY:

1. Mark a square on the floor with tape, or chalk if you are playing outside. Make sure it's big enough for all the players to sit in. This square is the "pound".

2. One child is the dogcatcher. They chase all the other children, who are "dogs". When they are tagged, the dog must go and sit in the pound.

3. If another child can reach the pound, they can free the dogs in there by touching them.

4. The game ends when the dogcatcher has put all the dogs in the pound. Then, the last dog caught becomes the new dogcatcher.

The dog pound

Lady is mistaken for a troublesome dog and taken to the pound. However, it isn't long before she's rescued by her owner's Aunt Sarah.

TOP TIP

Why not make a pair of dog ears on a paper band to wear while playing?

THE TIGGER MOVIE
Tigger Races

Tigger just loves to bounce. Although there's only one Tigger, you can join in, too. Spring into action and challenge your friends in this bouncing race.

You will need:

- Space hopper (Or bounce on your feet if you prefer!)

HOW TO PLAY:

1. Decide on a starting line and a finishing line.
2. Someone not taking part in the race shouts "Go!" and everyone bounces as fast as they can.
3. The first person over the finish line is the winner.
4. You could make the race harder by adding obstacles or other challenges.

SLEEPING BEAUTY
Sleeping Beauties

Calling all wannabe princesses and princes! It's time for an enchanted sleep. Pretend to doze in a fairy-tale castle in this royal party game.

You will need:

- Comfortable floor to lie on

HOW TO PLAY:

1. All but one player lies down on the floor. They must lie as still as they can with their eyes closed.
2. One person walks around looking for any sign of movement.
3. Whoever moves is out of the game.
4. If people are very still, the person patrolling can try to make them laugh by talking or doing silly things (but not touching them).
5. Whoever "sleeps" the longest is the winner.

TRY THIS!
Funny noises and silly voices can make the sleepers laugh.

Catch the Rat

Remy the rat has to be quick on his paws to stay hidden in the kitchen. He's used to sneaking around so no one knows where he is. See if your friends can find him with this fun game.

You will need:

- Cardboard tube
- Pencil
- Scissors
- Paintbrush
- Paint
- 3 paper cups

Making the rat

Create your own Remy to use in the game. Alternatively, you could use a small ball.

1 Draw a curved circle around the tube, about 7 cm (2½ in) high, with two ear shapes.

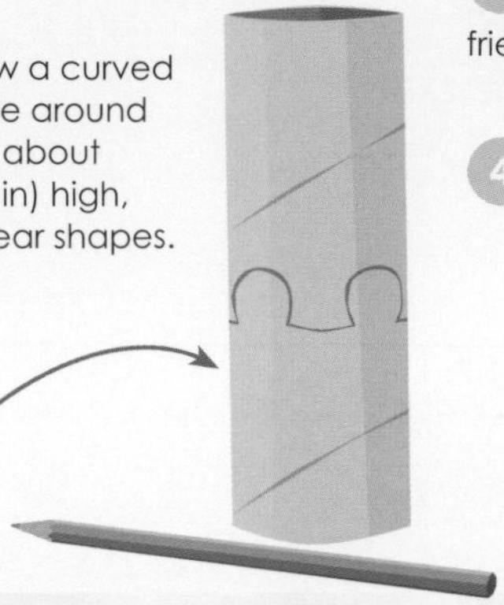

Check that your rat fits easily under a cup.

2 Carefully cut out the rat shape.

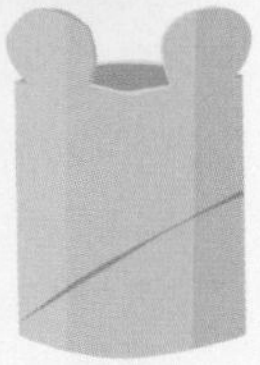

3 Use a pencil to draw Remy's friendly features.

4 Paint his face.

DID YOU KNOW?

Remy controls Linguini like a puppet. He pulls Linguini's hair, while hiding under his chef's hat.

HOW TO PLAY:

Place three identical cups and Remy in front of friends. Put a cup over the rat. Shuffle the cups. Move the cups quickly enough to fool your friends. Ask them which cup holds the rat. If they are right, they win!

White cups look like chefs' hats.

Pooh Sticks

When Winnie the Pooh accidentally dropped a pine cone into the river, the game Pooh Sticks was born. The animals of the Hundred-Acre Wood now play it all the time, and you can, too.

You will need:

- 1 stick for each player
- A bridge over running water

DID YOU KNOW?

Since 1984, there has been an Annual World Pooh Sticks Championship held in the UK.

Stick strategy

A smooth stick will travel faster, so remove any twigs or loose pieces of bark from your stick.

HOW TO PLAY:

1. Each player finds a stick to play with.

2. Players stand on a bridge, facing upriver.

3. All players hold their sticks at the same height, out over the water.

4. At the same moment, everyone drops their sticks into the water. Sticks should be dropped into the water, not thrown!

5. All players go to the other side of the bridge and look for their stick.

6. Whoever's stick appears from under the bridge first is the winner.

TOP TIP

Make sure everyone's sticks are easy to tell apart.

Fox and Hound Chase

Tod and Copper live in a world that says foxes and hounds are enemies. Challenge that idea, just like they do, with this chasing game.

You will need:

- An open space, free of obstacles

Star-crossed friends

As young pups, Tod and Copper don't think about the fact that they are meant to be enemies. Instead of chasing and hunting each other, they become the best of friends.

HOW TO PLAY:

1. One player is a "hound" and everyone else is a "fox", like Tod.

2. The hound chases all the players, and the first person they tag becomes "Copper".

3. The hound continues to chase the other foxes. When they are caught, the foxes must stand still with their arms and legs wide like a star shape.

4. Copper can choose to free the caught foxes by crawling through their legs.

5. Foxes can only be freed by Copper once. The second time they're caught, they stand with their legs together to show they're out of the game.

6. The game continues until all foxes are caught, apart from one, who is the winner.

Copper

Tod

DID YOU KNOW?

"Tod" is an old word for fox that was used mainly in Scotland.

101 Dalmatians Game

Dalmatians Pongo and Perdita set out to rescue their 15 puppies from the evil Cruella De Vil, but end up bringing home 101! Search for and rescue as many "dogs"as you can in this game of spots.

You will need:

- Protective floor covering (newspaper or plastic sheeting)
- White paper
- Black paint
- Old toothbrush
- Scissors

Get prepared
This is a game of hide-and-seek, but the first step is to prepare your "dogs".

1. Lay out white paper on newspaper or plastic sheeting.

2. Dip the toothbrush in black paint.

3. Hold the brush over the paper and rub the bristles so that paint flicks onto the paper, making a spotty pattern.

4. Once the paint is dry, cut out spotty circles – you can try and make it to 101!

TOP TIP
Remember how many "dogs" you have hidden, so you can keep track of your rescue mission.

HOW TO PLAY:

One person hides the spotty pieces of paper all around the room, house or garden. Everyone searches for the "dogs" as quickly as they can. The person who rescues the most dogs is the winner.

DID YOU KNOW?
Pongo uses the "Twilight Bark" – a special way of contacting other dogs across London – to help find his lost puppies.

Hiding places
The 101 captured puppies hide from Cruella and her henchmen in all sorts of strange places. They hide under a bed, under the stairs and in a moving van – they even roll in soot to disguise themselves!

Parachuting Soldiers

Attention! Your mission is to make your own *Toy Story* Green Army Men. Launch them from up high and watch them parachute back down to earth. Compete with your friends to see whose soldiers land first. Let's go, troops!

You will need:

- Tracing paper
- Pencil
- Green card
- Scissors
- Paper napkins
- Glue
- Hole punch
- String

Amass your army

The Green Army Men are professionals, but they still need the right gear for the job.

Make sure your holes are not punched too close to the edges.

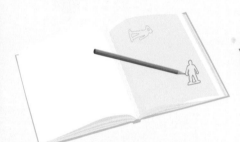

1 Trace the soldiers from the template on page 190, or design your own.

2 Copy the soldiers onto green card and cut them out. Each parachute needs two soldier shapes – a front and a back.

3 Open out your napkins to their full size. Punch a hole in each corner of the napkin.

Check that the threads are still the same length.

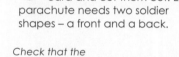

4 Cut two lengths of string 43 cm (17 in) long for each parachute.

5 Fold each string in half so that you have four smaller string pieces of equal length.

6 Glue the centre of both pieces of string to the back of a soldier. This will leave four ends of thread coming from the soldier.

7 Glue a second figure on the back of the soldier. This will cover up the loose ends and also make the soldier heavier for flight.

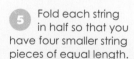

8 Thread each of the four string pieces through a hole and knot each one to secure. Now you're ready to fly!

Soldier's arm raised to attention

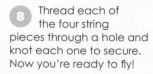

HOW TO PLAY:

Choose a soldier and stand at the top of a safe height. Let your soldiers go and watch them float safely down to the ground. The person whose soldier lands first wins!

You could use plain green napkins, or napkins decorated with army-style camouflage for undercover operations.

TOP TIP
To see what flies best, experiment with the size and weight of the napkin and the length of the strings.

Mulan's Training Camp

When Mulan joins the Emperor's army, she has to train very hard. Soldiers must be physically fit and strong to beat their enemies. Here's a game you can play that's perfect for warriors-in-training.

You will need:

- A crepe-paper streamer for each player, long enough to tie around their waist and hang down at least 30 cm (1 ft)

HOW TO PLAY:

1. Each player has a piece of crepe paper tied around their waist like a sash, with a strip hanging down.

2. The aim of the game is for each person to tear off as many sashes as possible without their own sash getting damaged.

3. The winner is the last remaining person with their sash intact.

4. You could play in teams with different-coloured sashes. Whichever team has the most sashes after a set amount of time wins.

TOP TIP
Tie the crepe paper loosely so it doesn't tear before you begin to play.

Brave warrior
At the army training camp, Mulan builds up her strength and fitness with hiking, running and climbing. She learns to fight using sticks, a bow and arrow and martial arts. She uses her skills to bring honour to her family by saving China!

SNOW WHITE AND THE SEVEN DWARFS
Apple Bobbing

TOP TIP
It's a good idea to wear goggles to protect your eyes!

Snow White is given a poisoned apple by her cruel stepmother that puts her into an enchanted sleep. But don't worry, the apples in this game are safe!

You will need:

- Large, clean tub
- Fresh water
- Apples
- Towels or plastic sheets

HOW TO PLAY:

1. Place all the apples in the tub about two-thirds full of water. It's best to play outside, but if you're inside, place the tub on towels or plastic sheets.

2. Each player takes a turn to put their hands behind their back and try to pick up an apple using only their mouth.

3. Once an apple has been bitten by someone, remove it from the water to keep the water clean.

4. The winner could be whoever picks up the most apples or whoever bites an apple the quickest.

TOY STORY
Toys Come Alive

Andy doesn't know it, but when he turns his back, the toys in his bedroom come alive. Step into the secret world of Buzz, Woody and friends with this fun game.

You will need:

- Music and music player

HOW TO PLAY:

1. One person is "Andy" and the other players are the "toys" in Andy's bedroom.

2. The music starts and the toys dance around.

3. Without warning, Andy stops the music. All toys must freeze, just like the toys do when a human comes into the room.

4. Whoever Andy judges to have moved after the music stops is out of the game.

5. The game continues until only one toy is left. They are the winner!

Who Am I?

There are hundreds of Disney characters, and you can choose your favourites for this guessing game. You can play anywhere – at parties, on car trips or at the dinner table.

You will need:

- Sticky notes
- Pens

HOW TO PLAY:

1. Each person writes the name of a Disney character on a sticky note – Bambi, for example.

2. Stick a note on each person's forehead. Make sure that no one sees who's on the paper on their own head.

3. Players take turns asking questions to work out which character they are. Questions must have a "yes" or "no" answer. For example, "Am I human?"

4. Each question earns the asker a point. The game ends when everyone has guessed their character. Whoever has the fewest points is the winner.

THE JUNGLE BOOK

Untangled

Mowgli discovers that there are many dangers in the jungle: fierce creatures, crumbling ruins and even plants to trip you up. See if you can escape from the jungle vines with this party game.

You will need:

- Crepe paper streamers (different colours for each team)

HOW TO PLAY:

1. Group all the players into teams.

2. Each team wraps a streamer around one person, from head to toe. Go carefully so the paper doesn't tear. Avoid covering anyone's nose or mouth.

3. Once someone in every team is caught up in the vines, the game can start.

4. The aim of the game is to rescue your teammate by untangling the paper as quickly as possible, without tearing it.

5. Whichever team has the streamer that is most intact at the end is the winner!

Memory Game

Riley's most powerful memories are about her family and friends. These memories are very important – Riley wouldn't be herself without them. Test your own memory with this challenge.

You will need:

- Card (white and coloured)
- Glue (optional) and scissors
- Coloured pens or pencils

DID YOU KNOW?

Riley's Long Term Memory holds over 17 billion shelves and has room for 1.2 trillion memories.

Design your cards

You'll need to have an even number of cards, with two of each image.

You could stick a patterned paper to the back of your cards.

1. Cut out rectangular pieces of card, all the same size.

2. Draw your own pictures. Make sure you have two of each picture.

3. Decorate the back of your cards. They should all look similar.

You could draw characters, objects, symbols or words.

HOW TO PLAY:

Mix up the cards and lay them in rows, face down. Turn over any two cards. If the two cards match, keep them. If they don't match, turn them back over. Try to remember what was on each card and where it was. Pay attention during the other players' turns, too. The game is over when all the cards have been matched. The player with the most pairs wins.

Archery Competition

How *Brave* are you? Unleash your inner Merida and stage your own Highland Games with an archery competition. This mini archery set is easy to make and is a great team game. Time to take aim!

You will need:

- Ice-lolly sticks
- Bowl of water
- Needle
- Large roll of tape
- Paint or felt-tip pens
- Dental floss
- Toothpicks
- PVA glue
- Cotton wool
- A round box with a lid
- Paint
- Paintbrush
- Coloured paper (optional)
- Scissors
- Thick thread
- Ink (optional)
- Protective covering

Prime your bow

You could make a single bow for everyone to share, or each archer could have a personalised one.

1. Soak the ice-lolly sticks in water for at least 30 minutes.

2. Ask an adult to make a hole in each end of the sticks with a needle.

3. Slowly bend the sticks into the inside of a large roll of tape. This will give them a curved shape.

4. Leave the sticks to dry inside the roll for at least an hour.

5. Decorate your bows with paint or felt-tip pens.

6. Knot one end of a piece of dental floss and thread it through one of the holes in the stick.

7. Wrap the floss around the stick and through the hole several times.

8. Once the floss is very secure, pull gently to make it taut, and thread it through the hole at the other end of the stick.

9. Wrap the thread around the stick and through the hole several times so it's secure, then knot it.

Prepare your arrows

Cotton swabs work well as arrows, but these plastic-free toothpicks are more environmentally friendly.

1. Carefully cut off one or both pointy ends of your toothpick with scissors, depending on the style.

2. Dip one end in glue.

3. Take a small piece of cotton wool and twist it around the tip.

4. Fluff the cotton wool to make it more round.

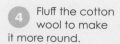

TRY THIS! For a fun clan competition, each team can make up their own clan name and colours. Create a scoreboard to keep track of the winner!

Mark your target

Archery targets are round, with coloured rings and a bullseye in the centre. The bigger your target, the easier the game will be.

1. Paint the lid of a round cardboard box with white paint.

2. Add coloured rings. You could paint them or glue down rings of coloured paper.

3. Ask an adult to pierce two holes in the side of the main part of the box using a needle or pencil.

4. Push thread through the holes to make a loop for hanging.

5. Tie a knot in each end of the thread to secure it.

6. Put the lid back on the box and hang it up.

HOW TO PLAY:

Give each player paint or ink in their clan colour. Before firing, each archer dips their arrow in the paint or ink so it will leave a mark on the target. Make sure you put down a covering to protect the floor. Whoever's mark lands nearest to the centre of the target is the winner.

Dental floss is wrapped many times to make it secure.

Test Your Knowledge!

There are many magical worlds full of fantastic facts in Disney and Disney•Pixar movies. Put your knowledge to the test with these quizzes covering everything from dalmatians and dragons to talking cars and flying elephants. Good luck!

Definitively Disney
Challenge yourself with these questions on classic Disney movies – from *101 Dalmatians* and *Bambi* to *Hercules* and *Peter Pan*.

The Jungle Book
1 What does King Louis ask Mowgli to teach him?
A: How to sing
B: How to make fire
C: How to make friends

Bambi
2 What was Bambi's first word?

A: Bird   **B**: Mother   **C**: Butterfly

The Jungle Book
3 Who hypnotises Mowgli with his eyes?

A: Baloo   **B**: Kaa   **C**: Bagheera

Big Hero 6
4 What is the name of Hiro's brother?
A: GoGo
B: Baymax
C: Tadashi

Dumbo
5 What does Dumbo use to fly?
A: His trunk
B: His tail
C: His ears

101 Dalmatians
6 What animal is Sergeant Tibbs?
A: Horse
B: Dog
C: Cat

Aladdin
7 What is Aladdin's name when he turns into a prince?
A: Ali Ambibi
B: Ali Ababwa
C: Ali Abubu

Alice in Wonderland
8 What is the name of Alice's cat?
A: Dinah
B: Mary
C: Kitty

The Lion King
9 Which one of these is NOT one of Scar's hyena followers?
A: Shenzi
B: Ed
C: Kevin

The Aristocats
10 Which alley cat helps Duchess and her kittens find their way home?
A: Thomas O'Malley
B: Edgar Balthazar
C: Frou-Frou

The Sword in the Stone
11 What is the name of the wizard?
A: Greybeard
B: Merlin
C: Arthur

Pinocchio
12 Before Pinocchio becomes a real boy, what is he?
A: A doll
B: A statue
C: A puppet

Hercules
13 Who trains Hercules to be a hero?
A: Phil
B: James
C: Tom

Fantasia
14 What object does Mickey Mouse enchant to carry water?
A: A rubbish bin
B: A broom
C: A sponge

Peter Pan
15 Which one of these is NOT one of The Lost Boys?

A: Cubby   **B**: Mr. Smee   **C**: Slightly

Perfectly Pixar

Do you know your Luigi from your Linguini? Test yourself to see how good your Pixar knowledge really is with this quiz.

The Incredibles

1 What is Helen Parr's superpower?
A: Making herself invisible
B: Stretching her body into any shape
C: Running super fast

Coco

2 What is banned in Miguel Rivera's family home?
A: Music
B: Reading
C: Painting

Cars

3 Who is Lightning McQueen's best friend?
A: Holly Shiftwell
B: Doc Hudson
C: Mater

Finding Nemo

4 Who helps Nemo ride the gnarly waves of the East Australian Current?

A: Crush
B: Bruce
C: Gill

Finding Dory

5 Which grouchy octopus is actually a septopus?
A: Hank
B: Larry
C: Bill

Toy Story

6 What is written on the bottom of Woody's boot?
A: Woody
B: Andy
C: Jessie

Inside Out

7 What colour are Riley's scary memories?
A: Purple
B: Red
C: Yellow

Ratatouille

8 Who inspires Remy to cook?

A: Alfredo Linguini
B: Auguste Gusteau
C: Anton Ego

Toy Story

9 What's the name of Andy's nightmare neighbour?
A: Sid
B: Ned
C: Seth

Brave

10 How many brothers does Merida have?
A: One
B: Two
C: Three

Monsters, Inc.

11 What do monster scarers travel through to collect children's screams?
A: Windows
B: Portals
C: Doors

Up

12 Which Wilderness Explorer travels with Carl?
A: Russell
B: Eddy
C: John

The Good Dinosaur

13 Where does Apatosaurus Arlo first meet Spot?
A: In a cave
B: By a river
C: On his farm

Cars

14 Which car loves giving paint makeovers to other cars?

A: Flo
B: Luigi
C: Ramone

A Bug's Life

15 Which evil grasshopper terrifies an ant colony?
A: Hopper
B: Cruncher
C: Banger

Answers

p75 : 1.B, 2.A, 3.C, 4.A, 5.A, 6.B, 7.B, 8.B, 9.A, 10.C, 11.C, 12.A, 13.C, 14.C, 15.A
p74 : 1.B, 2.A, 3.B, 4.C, 5.C, 6.C, 7.B, 8.A, 9.C, 10.A, 11.B, 12.C, 13.A, 14.B, 15.B

ART

Mickey String Decoration

Mickey Mouse is loved all around the world. He is so famous, he can be recognised just by the shape of his ears! This eye-catching string art makes the most of Mickey's best features.

You will need:

- 3 small balloons
- Coloured string
- Scissors
- PVA glue
- Water
- Bowl
- Spoon for mixing
- Newspaper
- Glitter
- Tweezers
- Drawing pin
- Thin ribbon

Prepare the balloons

The shape of Mickey's head and ears is built using three balloons as a base. These are popped and removed later.

1 Blow up one balloon so that it's about the size of your fist. This will be Mickey's head.

2 Blow up two more balloons, smaller than the head, for Mickey's ears.

3 Tie some string around the neck of each balloon. You will use this to hold the balloon when it is covered in glue.

Prepare the string

A simple mixture of glue and water coats the string so it sticks to the balloons and then dries into a fixed shape.

Keep holes large enough to pull out the balloon.

1 Cut your string into pieces about 50 cm (20 in) long.

2 Mix equal amounts of PVA glue and water in a bowl.

3 Dip a piece of string into the glue mixture so that it is entirely covered.

4 Wrap the wet string round and round your balloon, making a criss-cross pattern. Repeat until the three balloons are covered with string.

Bring it all together

Once your balloons are covered with string, you can add some sparkle, then join them together.

1 While the string is still wet, hold your balloon over newspaper and sprinkle glitter over it.

Excess glitter is caught on the newspaper.

2 Add glitter to the other balloons in the same way.

3 Hang up the balloons to dry overnight. Lay newspaper underneath in case they drip.

4 Once the balloons are dry, push tweezers through gaps in the string to gently separate the balloon from the string.

5 Carefully use a drawing pin to pop the balloon.

6 Carefully remove the balloon with tweezers. Discard the broken pieces.

Glue under each ear and attach to the head.

7 Glue the three balls together.

8 Tie a ribbon on the large ball and hang up your Mickey decoration.

Find the right spot to tie your ribbon so the decoration hangs balanced.

These decorations are about 15 cm (6 in) wide.

DID YOU KNOW?
Mickey Mouse's birthday is November 18th. This is the day he first appeared in a cartoon in 1928.

MOANA
Story Stones

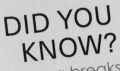

In Moana's home of Motunui, stories are very important. The islanders tell the stories of their elders to remind them who they are and where they are from. Use these stones to tell your own exciting stories.

You will need:

- Stones
- Acrylic paint
- Paintbrush
- PVA glue
- Bag or other container

Make your story stones

These stones tell the story of Moana's amazing adventures. You can paint pictures to tell your own tale!

 1 Make sure your stones are clean and dry.

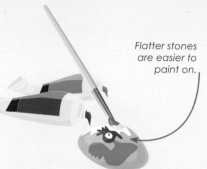

Flatter stones are easier to paint on.

 2 Paint pictures on the stones with acrylic paint.

 3 Once the paint is dry, varnish with PVA glue. Leave to dry, then let your storytelling begin!

HOW TO PLAY:

Choose a stone from the bag and start a story based on its picture. Another stone is taken from the bag and the story continues. One person can tell the whole story, or you can pass the bag to your friends to carry on the tale.

TOP TIP
Use a toothpick or the end of your paintbrush to add small details to your stones.

Tropical flower

Maui's magical fishhook

Pacific island

Red stingray

Kakamora pirate

Heart of Te Fiti

Moana's sailboat

Heihei the rooster

THE ARISTOCATS
Button Art

Isn't Marie from *The Aristocats* as cute as a button? Especially when she's made into this button artwork! You can create beautiful pictures out of buttons using Marie or any other character you like.

You will need:

- White paper
- Pencil
- Scissors
- Buttons
- Felt
- PVA glue
- Coloured card

DID YOU KNOW?
Marie is a white Turkish Angora kitten. She lives in France with her mother, Duchess, and her two brothers.

Turn buttons into art

Choose a pose of a character to remake in buttons. Marie's big pink bow acts as perfect contrast to her white fur.

Silhouette is a single colour.

1 Draw the outline of your chosen character on white paper and cut it out.

A large button is perfect in the middle of the bow.

2 Lay buttons on the paper and move them around until you like the arrangement.

3 Glue each button down carefully. If you have trouble sticking them to the paper, glue them onto felt shapes first.

Marie's ears and nose work well as pink highlights.

4 Cut shapes out of felt for highlights and glue them to the paper.

5 Stick your picture on coloured card. Once it is dry, you could frame it.

Layer up buttons for variety.

81

Paint-Splatter Fireworks

When Mulan defeats the Hun leader, she sets off a tower full of fireworks. The whole Imperial City watches the display! Create your own dazzling fireworks show with paint.

You will need:

- Scrap paper
- Black or dark-blue paper
- Reusable plastic straw
- Paint in different colours
- Paintbrush
- Glitter (optional)
- Red paper (optional)
- Glue (optional)

Light up your picture

This paint-splatter technique uses a straw and your own breath to create a unique pattern.

1 First of all, practise blowing paint on a piece of scrap paper. If your paint is too thick, add water to make it thinner.

2 Drop a small spot of paint onto your paper using a paintbrush.

3 Hold the straw over the spot of paint.

4 Blow through the straw to spread out the paint.

5 Experiment with different ways of breathing on scrap paper. Generally, short, sharp blows of air work best for firework shapes.

You could add glitter on top of your fireworks.

6 Wash your straw out before changing paint colour.

7 Once you're happy with the shapes you're getting, repeat these steps on your final paper.

8 Repeat as many times as you want, using different colours of paint.

9 You could cut a silhouette shape, such as the Imperial Palace, out of paper and glue it to the foreground of your picture.

DID YOU KNOW?

Fireworks were invented in China.

TRY THIS!

Why not make this type of picture to celebrate Chinese New Year?

Papel Picado

Miguel Rivera and his family decorate their home for the festival Día de los Muertos (Day of the Dead). Take inspiration from the traditional Mexican craft of papel picado to make these colourful paper flags.

You will need:

- Sheets of paper in bright colours
- Ruler
- Pencil
- Scissors
- String
- Double-sided tape

Designing your own

Folding your paper in half before you cut creates symmetrical designs for your papel picado.

Use a ruler to make your folds neat.

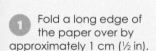

1 Fold a long edge of the paper over by approximately 1 cm (½ in).

Remember that your design will be reversed on the other half of the paper.

2 Fold your piece of paper in half. Draw your design with a pencil on one half.

3 Cut out the shapes and then unfold your paper.

4 Use double-sided tape to attach the string in the crease on the back of the paper. Fold the top edge of the paper back over onto the tape.

String will be hidden under the fold.

TOP TIP
Leave enough space between cut-out shapes to keep the paper strong.

Designs can be pictures or patterns.

You can shape the edges of the paper, too.

Personalised Letters

Transform your bedroom with a touch of Disney Princess magic! Spell out your name with cardboard letters and embellish each one to make it even more enchanting.

Make your letters

For each of these letters, a different princess has been depicted. But you can choose anything you like. These steps use pre-made 3D letters, but you could also cut your letters out of flat card.

You will need:

- Pre-made cardboard letters
- Paper
- Coloured pencils or pens
- Scissors
- Glue or double-sided tape
- Coloured paper
- Felt, jewels, sequins (optional)
- Paint and paintbrush

1 On paper, plan out your designs. Think about the clothing, features or accessories that best represent the character you have chosen.

2 Paint each letter in a base colour. You could stick coloured paper onto each letter with glue or double-sided tape instead.

Distinctive sleeves

Flower from forest

Mulan

Snow White

Aurora

A green base matches Mulan's sleeves perfectly.

Pieces of coloured paper are layered to create Mulan's look.

TRY THIS!
What about making your name out of decorated letters and sticking them on your bedroom door?

3   If you have used paint on the letters, wait for it to dry. Use the cardboard letters as a template to work out the size each piece of your design will need to be. Draw your shapes on coloured paper.

4   Carefully cut out the shapes and stick them onto the letters with glue or double-sided tape.

You could add extra details with decorations such as felt, jewels or sequins.

Headband with sapphire jewel

Turquoise gem necklace

Fringed clothing

Pocahontas

Ariel

Jasmine

Handprint Fish

Nemo wants to explore away from his home in the Great Barrier Reef, but his father wants him to stay close and be safe. Bring the ocean to you with this fun painting technique.

You will need:

- Safe, washable paint
- Thick paintbrush
- Fine paintbrush
- White paper
- Black felt-tip pen
- Scissors
- PVA glue
- Googly eye
- Card or craft foam

Print with your hand

Work quickly when painting on your hand so the pattern is complete before the paint dries.

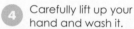

1 Paint white stripes directly onto your palm with a thick paintbrush.

2 Paint the rest of your hand orange, avoiding the white stripes, so it looks like the orange and white stripes of a clownfish.

3 Place your hand onto white paper. Press down all the parts of your hand, being careful not to smudge the paint.

4 Carefully lift up your hand and wash it.

TRY THIS!
Make two pictures – one could be Nemo and the other could be his dad, Marlin, when they're trying to reunite.

5 Once the paint is dry, cut out the hand shape.

6 Add details with a black pen or black paint and a fine paintbrush.

7 Glue on a googly eye.

8 Prepare a home for your fish by painting a sheet of card or craft foam. You could add details such as underwater plants or bubbles.

9 Glue the fish to your final picture.

DID YOU KNOW?
There are more than 25 different species of clownfish living in seas all over the world!

You could decorate your picture with real shells.

Stained-Glass Windows

Quasimodo, known as the Hunchback of Notre Dame, lives in Paris's large cathedral. Take inspiration from Notre Dame's spectacular stained-glass windows to make luminous artworks.

You will need:

- Black paper
- White pencil
- Ruler (optional)
- Scissors
- Coloured cellophane
- Glue stick

Create your window design

Traditionally, stained-glass windows are held together using lead. Black paper will give you the same effect.

Stained-glass designs are usually symmetrical.

1 Draw your design in white pencil on black paper.

2 Your windows can be any shape you like. If you'd prefer them to be geometrical, use a ruler to help you.

3 Carefully cut out the shapes you've drawn. Ask an adult to help with the smaller inner sections.

Add coloured glass

Coloured cellophane is transparent enough for light to shine through. When put against a sunny window, your shapes will glow like coloured glass.

You can have one colour of cellophane for each hole, or you can overlap different pieces so that the colours merge together.

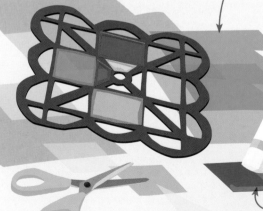

Glue around the edges of the cellophane.

TOP TIP
Make the paper lines between the window shapes quite thick. This will keep your picture stable.

1 Cut up pieces of brightly coloured cellophane.

2 Use a glue stick to glue the cellophane over the holes, on the back of the black paper.

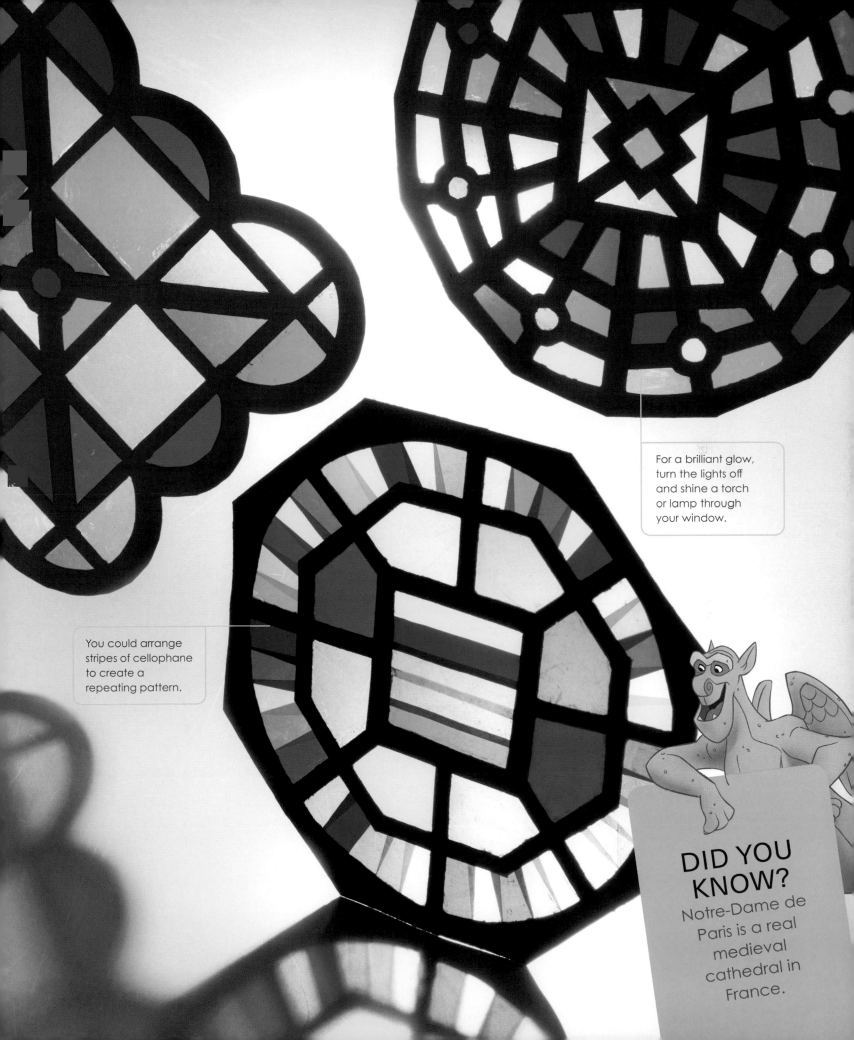

For a brilliant glow, turn the lights off and shine a torch or lamp through your window.

You could arrange stripes of cellophane to create a repeating pattern.

DID YOU KNOW?
Notre-Dame de Paris is a real medieval cathedral in France.

Let there be light
Just like the stained-glass windows in the real Notre-Dame de Paris Cathedral, your designs will create colourful patterns when light shines through them.

Pixel Art

Images on computers and video games are made up of tiny blocks of colour called pixels. Turn your pictures into pixelated artworks with help from video-game star Wreck-It Ralph.

You will need:

- Graph paper
- Pencil
- Rubber
- Felt-tip pens or crayons

Get pixelated

It's easy to turn any picture into pixels with graph paper. Just follow these simple steps.

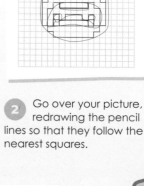

1 Draw your picture in pencil on graph paper, ignoring the squares. Press lightly, as you will be rubbing out these lines later.

2 Go over your picture, redrawing the pencil lines so that they follow the nearest squares.

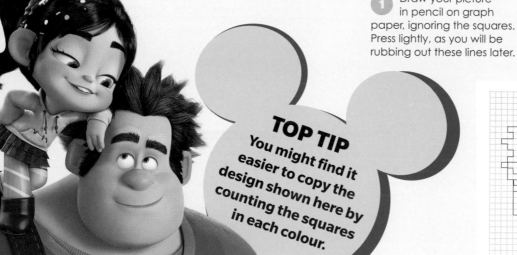

TOP TIP
You might find it easier to copy the design shown here by counting the squares in each colour.

3 When you're happy with the new design, rub out any unnecessary pencil lines.

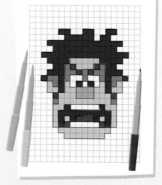

4 Colour your picture in, filling in only whole squares.

5 Colour in the background, keeping to the squares.

Scale everything from the pupil of Ralph's eye, which is one square in size.

DID YOU KNOW?
Wreck-It Ralph destroys everything, but he wants to be accepted as a good guy.

Concertina Cards

Dress your cards to impress with these fancy ball gowns. Pop-up cards are easy to make with this crafty technique. You will soon have 3D princesses bursting out of your greetings cards.

You will need:

- Tracing paper
- Coloured card
- Pencil
- Scissors
- Glue stick
- Double-sided tape

Dress up your cards

The 3D skirts are made by cutting several skirts and sticking them together.

1 Draw or trace the silhouette of your favourite princess onto coloured card, such as silver. Carefully cut it out.

Match this card to the princess's dress colour.

2 Using the silhouette as a template, draw out just the dress on a different-coloured card. Cut it out.

3 Copy the skirt part of the dress onto the dress-colour card four times and cut them out.

You could cut the edge of the card to make a decorative pattern.

A head turned to the side makes a better silhouette than one facing forwards.

Tiana

Sleeping Beauty

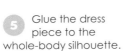

4 Fold all the pieces in half. Use the silhouette piece as a guide for the other pieces.

5 Glue the dress piece to the whole-body silhouette.

6 Attach the folded skirt pieces to each other with double-sided tape along the inside folds.

7 Glue the skirt pieces to the dress, matching up the folds.

Rectangular pieces keep the skirts evenly spaced.

8 Cut nine small rectangles of card and fold them into four equal sections.

9 Glue one rectangle inside each fold of the skirts.

10 Fold a larger rectangle of card in half. You could decorate it.

11 Glue the princess inside the card, once again matching up the centre folds.

TOP TIP
Use the dress piece as a template to trace around when you draw the four skirts.

Belle

Cinderella

Abstract Art

Joy, Sadness and Bing Bong pass through Abstract Thought – an area of Riley's mind where objects (and characters!) are transformed into simple shapes. See if you can simplify your drawings with these two abstract art techniques.

You will need:

- Different-coloured card or paper
- Pens or pencils
- Scissors
- Glue

Create a collage

Joy, Sadness and Bing Bong become a colourful collection of flat shapes. You can simplify any 3D object by breaking it down into basic shapes. Collaging different papers is a simple way of creating this effect.

Joy's hair becomes a simple triangle.

Each character is made up of multiple shapes.

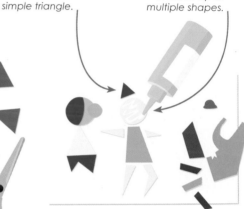

1 Use coloured pencils or pens to plan the simplified shapes you will need.

2 Cut out all the shapes.

3 Stick the shapes down on a background of your choice. It is helpful to arrange your shapes before you stick them down.

Go super simple

As they spend longer in Abstract Thought, Joy, Sadness and Bing Bong become single shapes. See if you can show your objects as single shapes, too.

Bing Bong's trunk shape and pink colouring are instantly recognisable.

1 Draw your shape on coloured paper and cut it out.

2 Arrange them on a background. You could also add other characters, or objects drawn as single shapes, to make a scene.

DID YOU KNOW?

Bing Bong is an imaginary friend Riley created when she was a toddler. He is part-cat, part-elephant, part-dolphin and is made of candy floss!

TRY THIS!
See what your friends and family would look like as simple shapes.

Collection of shapes
Joy, Sadness and Bing Bong try to reach for the door that seems to be floating away.

Sliding Image

Carl Fredricksen uses 10,000 balloons to turn his beloved house into a flying machine. Turn your hand to an adventurous paper engineering technique that will take your imagination up, up and away!

Make the pictures

Where in the world would you like to travel? You could try using landscapes of places you'd like to visit for your own adventure book, just as Carl Fredricksen did.

You could use magazine images to create your scene.

1 Draw a house held up by balloons on plain paper and cut it out.

2 Draw or make a collage for the background picture on one of the pieces of card.

Make the pictures

The balloon house travels up the card in a channel cut in the top layer. It's held in place by two coins connected by foam.

1.5 cm (½ in)

1 Draw a channel on your background picture 1.5 cm (½ in) wide.

2 Ask an adult to help cut out the channel with a craft knife or scissors.

3 Using double-sided foam tape, stick a coin to the back of the balloons.

4 Cut an extra piece of foam tape slightly smaller than the width of the channel.

5 Stick the foam onto the top side of the coin.

6 Position the card over the balloon picture, with the foam piece in the channel.

7 Stick the second coin onto the foam.

8 Check that the foam can move freely along the channel. Trim if needed.

Add the back panel

Hide the workings of your picture and make it neat by backing it with a second piece of card. This will also make your artwork more stable.

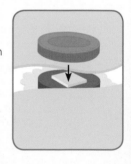

1 Place double-sided foam tape all around the edges of the back of the card.

2 Stick the back panel on top of the original card.

TOP TIP
Use thick card. It will need to stand up to the constant sliding and weight of the coins.

Balloon picture slides up and down.

Carl collected images of places he wanted to visit in his adventure book.

DID YOU KNOW?

Six-year-old Russell accidentally ends up on the house-flying adventure with 78-year-old Carl Fredricksen!

Balloon Faces

There's lots to celebrate when Nick and Judy solve the biggest mystery in Zootropolis. Add some animal magic to your own celebration with these distinctive balloons.

You will need:

- Tracing paper
- Pencil
- Paper
- Coloured pens or pencils
- Scissors
- Balloon
- Glue stick
- Sticky tape
- Ribbon

Clawhauser

Decorate a balloon

These instructions are for Dawn Bellwether. You can find a template at the back of this book. You can also take inspiration from Zootropolis's many characters and design your own balloon faces using the same steps.

1 Trace the template on page 193 onto tracing paper.

2 Copy the shapes onto paper and cut them all out.

3 Colour in the facial features and add any details.

Dawn Bellwether

4 Blow up and tie a balloon.

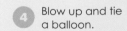

5 Use glue to stick the facial features onto the balloon.

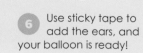

6 Use sticky tape to add the ears, and your balloon is ready!

Pick a coloured balloon to match the character's fur – or wool!

Nick Wilde

TOP TIP
A tab behind the ears folded and stuck to the balloon makes the ears stand upright.

Judy Hopps

Drooping eyelids show Flash's slow nature.

Flash

DID YOU KNOW?
Deputy Mayor Bellwether doesn't just have her own woolly coat – she will only ever wear clothing made from wool.

103

Slotted Sculptures

Give old cardboard a new life with this eco-friendly art project. Combine simple shapes to make your own Mickey and Daisy sculptures, which can be taken apart and put back together again and again.

You will need:

- Tracing paper
- Pencil
- Corrugated cardboard
- Scissors
- Acrylic paint
- Felt-tip pens

Get prepared

Take care copying the template, especially the slots. If your pieces aren't quite straight, your models might be wobbly and fall over.

1 Trace the templates on pages 194–195 onto tracing paper.

2 Copy the shapes onto cardboard and cut them out.

3 Cut along the lines to create slots in each piece.

Add some colour

Once all the parts are cut out, they're ready to decorate.

You could use white paint to add buttons to Mickey's trousers.

1 Paint all of the shapes. Acrylic paint covers cardboard well.

2 Add details on the faces. You can paint these or use felt-tip pens.

3 Leave the pieces to dry.

4 Slot the pieces together to build your sculpture.

Sculpting Daisy

Here are the pieces you need for Daisy. Remember to make two feet and two hands!

TRY THIS!

Challenge your friends to put the sculptures together blindfolded!

DID YOU KNOW?

Daisy Duck and her best friend Minnie Mouse run a bow-tique together.

Each piece sits at right angles to the piece next to it.

Make sure that the bottom of the feet are cut straight so that your figures stand up!

105

ACTIVITIES

Grass-Hair Trolls

Grow some crazy grass hair on your own meddlesome *Frozen* Trolls. These little guys care very much about Kristoff and Anna. Now it's your turn to take care of them. Add a little water each day and watch them come to life!

You will need:

- Scissors
- Craft foam
- Felt
- Coloured beads
- Black cotton thread
- An old pair of tights
- Small elastic bands
- Plate

- 300 g (10 oz) compost per troll
- Grass seed
- Craft glue
- Googly eyes
- Black permanent marker

Prepare your Troll

Cut arms, ears and feet from brown craft foam, and eyebrows, a cape and a collar from green felt.

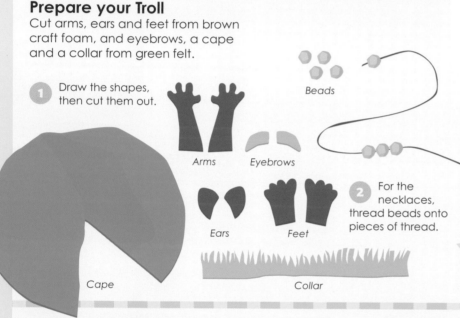

1 Draw the shapes, then cut them out.

Arms

Eyebrows

Beads

2 For the necklaces, thread beads onto pieces of thread.

Ears

Feet

Cape

Collar

Shape the body

Your Troll will gain its lumpy, rounded shape when filled with compost!

3 Tie the top loosely with an elastic band.

1 Cut one leg of the tights to your desired Troll height, with some extra to spare.

2 Pour in the compost, pushing it to the bottom of the tights.

4 Separate the bundle into a head and body with an elastic band.

6 Reopen the top to add 1 tbsp grass seed, before retying.

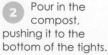

5 Pull out a little nose from the head and tie another band around it.

Grass seed

Troll assembly

Now it's time to personalise your Troll. When sticking on the features, you will need to hold the felt down until the glue is fully dry.

Eyebrows

Ears

Eyes

Arms

Feet

1 Add a little smile and eyelashes with a black marker.

2 Glue on all the felt pieces and googly eyes.

3 Tie the beaded necklace around the neck.

4 Wrap the cape around the Troll, sticking the sides down so that it doesn't jut out.

5 Glue the collar in place over the top of the cape and leave it to dry.

6 Put the Troll on a plate in a sunny place and add a little water each day. You should see hair sprout after about 4 days!

Give your Troll a cool haircut! How about a mohican?

TOP TIP
If you don't have compost or grass seed, try cotton wool and garden cress seeds instead!

Avoid putting grass seed in the face area – unless you want a Troll with facial hair!

Add extra decoration, such as this belt made from thread, tied with a simple knot.

Mushu Shadow Puppet

Mushu the tiny dragon knows the power of his shadow. When he reveals himself to Mulan, he uses it to seem much bigger and fiercer than he is. He's the perfect character for a shadow puppet!

You will need:

- Tracing paper
- Pencil
- Scissors
- Red card
- Hole punch
- Split pin
- Wooden dowels
- Sticky tape
- A light, such as a torch or a lamp

Prepare your puppet

Storytelling with shadow puppets is an ancient tradition. Once you've made Mushu, you can perform endless shows.

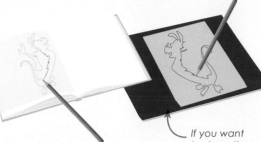

If you want to strengthen your puppet, glue extra layers of card to your shapes.

1 Trace the templates on page 198 and copy them onto red card. Carefully cut the pieces out.

2 Use a hole punch to make a single hole in the top of each arm and the shoulder of the main body.

You can reposition the dowels to get different movements from your puppet.

3 Push the split pin through the front of the body piece and the arm pieces, then open and flatten out the splits.

4 Tape wooden dowels to the two hands.

Split pin allows arms to move separately from the body.

Experiment with the distances of the puppet and light source from the wall.

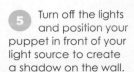

5 Turn off the lights and position your puppet in front of your light source to create a shadow on the wall.

6 Practise using the dowels to manipulate the puppet – then you're ready to perform!

Thin dowels won't cast much of a shadow – leaving Mushu the star of the show.

You could create a sillhouette scene for your shadow play.

DID YOU KNOW?
Mushu was once a guardian spirit for Mulan's family, but he lost that honour. He regains his place as a guardian by helping Mulan.

Scavenger Hunt

You can draw on all your favourite characters for this game. It's a scavenger hunt that combines your friends' knowledge of Disney with their ability to find objects against the clock.

You will need:

- An area to play in that's full of interesting objects
- Paper
- Pens

DID YOU KNOW?

In a Donald Duck story from 1954, Donald helps his nephews Huey, Dewey and Louie win a scavenger hunt competition.

Write your clues

Compile a list for scavengers based on what's available to you. Here are some sample suggestions to get you started:

HOW TO PLAY:

1. Write a list of clues for objects that can be found in the area you're playing in – such as your house or a park. Clues could either be physical objects or photographs.

2. People can play individually or, if there are more than three or four players, in teams.

3. Each team has the same list of clues. The aim of the game is to find as many items on the list as quickly as possible.

4. There are a few ways to play. The winner could be the team that finds the most items from the list in a set time or the team that finds all the items first.

5. You could also use the clues to make a treasure hunt. Set up each clue to lead to the next clue, and finally a hidden prize.

Clue: A bear of very little brain would eat this all day long if he could.
Answer: Honey

Clue: A line of these guides Dory home.
Answer: Shells

Clue: Lady and the Tramp share this type of pasta.
Answer: Spaghetti

Create a Secret Club

When Mike and Sulley go to Monsters University, they join a fraternity. Fraternities and sororities are a bit like secret clubs. Why not create your own, invite your friends to join, and let them in on the secrets!

You will need:

- Paper
- Coloured felt-tip pens

TOP TIP
Fraternities and sororities do a lot of charity work. Is there anything your club can do to help people?

Setting up your club

Mike and Sulley join the fraternity called Oozma Kappa ("OK"), with team colours in green and yellow. You could set up your own team to compete in your very own Scare Games.

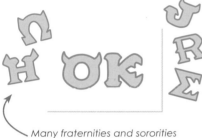

Many fraternities and sororities use the Greek alphabet to make their names.

Rules:

1 Choose a name for your club.

2 Make rules for your club, such as always wearing green clothes.

3 Design a logo and make badges or banners.

4 Make membership cards for everyone.

DID YOU KNOW?

Mike and Sulley go to study at Monsters University because they both want to be Scarers at Monsters, Inc. when they're grown up.

113

Ursula's Bath Bombs

Create your own bath bombs that will bubble and fizz in your tub, just like one of Ursula's potions! But don't worry: they don't release magic, just fizz, fragrance and relaxation!

You will need:

- Two mixing bowls
- 80 g (3 oz) cream of tartar
- 360 g (12½ oz) bicarbonate of soda
- 15–25 drops of essential oil
- 10–15 drops of soap dye or food colouring
- A tiny bit of water

- Spray bottle
- Gloves (optional)
- Moulds or muffin tray
- Sieve
- 1 tbsp of carrier oil such as olive or apricot oil (optional, for moisturising)
- Cling film

Prepare your potions

You don't need ingredients from the bottom of the sea for your potion, just common household items. These measurements will make a batch of bath bombs.

Use ingredients that are gentle to your skin. Avoid contact with your face and eyes.

1 Combine the cream of tartar and bicarbonate of soda in a mixing bowl. You might want to wear gloves when handling any ingredients.

2 Sift the powders back and forth between two bowls to mix them thoroughly.

Essential oil

Soap dye or food colouring

Carrier oil

Water

For moisture as well as fizz, add carrier oil at this stage.

3 Add 15–25 drops of essential oil (depending on the strength of the blend).

4 Add 10–15 drops of soap dye or food colouring (depending on the shade of colour you want).

5 Quickly mix the potion with your hands before it has a chance to fizz. As you mix, spray in water, a tiny bit at a time. Break up any lumps.

6 Continue until the mixture just holds its shape when squeezed, but is still a little crumbly.

Get moulding

Novelty moulds can give you interesting-shaped bath bombs, but you could also use a muffin tray for simpler shapes.

Create a marbled effect by layering different coloured batches in the moulds.

To protect the mould, line it with cling film first.

1 Pack the mixture tightly into your moulds.

2 If you're using a two-part mould, slightly overfill each half and press them together tightly, without twisting.

3 Let your bath bombs dry for a couple of hours in a warm, dry place. Keep them out of direct sunlight.

4 Once the bath bombs are dry, carefully push them out of the mould – then they are ready for bathtime!

TOP TIP
Bath bombs lose their fizz over time, so use yours within a few weeks.

DID YOU KNOW?
Ursula is a scheming sea witch who deceives Ariel and tries to take over King Triton's underwater kingdom.

Bath bombs make great gifts.

Nautical shapes suit the undersea theme.

Baymax Origami

Baymax is a big, inflatable personal health-care companion who can fold back down into his small carry case. Make a different type of folding Baymax using the Japanese art of folding paper known as origami.

You will need:

- A square piece of white paper
- Scissors
- Black pen

Fold your way to success

Don't worry if you don't fold it right first time. Practise on scrap paper before you make your final Baymax.

Fold along the line as shown.

Your paper will now have eight fold marks in it.

1 Fold a square of paper in half to make a triangle. Then fold left corner to right corner, and unfold.

2 Now fold the paper in half into a rectangle. Open out and fold again the opposite way.

3 Holding the paper on the folds, at the marks shown, bring your hands towards each other until all corners of the paper meet in the middle.

4 Fold the flap in front to the right and the flap behind to the left. Flatten the base well to make a square.

5 Rotate your square so the open flaps are at the bottom. Fold flaps A and B into the centre. Flatten, then unfold.

6 Fold the top corner down. Crease well, then unfold.

7 Lift the front flap of the model, bring it upwards, and push the sides of the model inwards at the same time. Flatten the model down, creasing well.

This is the beginning of Baymax's body shape.

Your model should now look like a thin diamond, with the top part of the diamond split open.

Make sure this triangle points downwards.

8 Turn the model over and repeat steps 5 to 7 on the other side. Then rotate your model 180 degrees.

9 Open the model by folding point C to point D.

10 Turn the model over and repeat step 9 on the other side.

11 To make the legs, fold the lower two points up to meet the base of the downwards facing triangle. Unfold and then fold the legs up inside the model.

TOP TIP
To turn a rectangular piece of paper into a square, fold one corner across to the opposite side to make a triangle and cut off the excess.

Add some detail

Now that you have the basic body shape, you can start adding Baymax's arms and legs – as well as his friendly face.

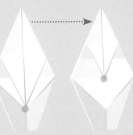

1 To make arms, fold the top flap down to the two points shown to mark two creases.

2 On the front piece only, cut up to the middle point between the two creased lines.

3 Fold each arm back on itself at a 45-degree angle, so they both stick out at the sides.

4 To make the head, fold down the back flap to just above the shoulder line.

5 Fold the flap back up and open out the head flap to the two points shown.

6 Fold the head over and flatten down.

7 To make Baymax's chin, fold up the bottom corner of the face, then fold under.

8 Fold the ends of the arms backwards to make hands.

9 Draw Baymax's face, and he's ready to go!

Fairy-Tale Castle

Use mathematical magic to transform plain card into a spectacular castle! Flat shapes called nets fold up to become 3D blocks for building your own fairy-tale structure.

You will need:

- Tracing paper
- Pencil
- Coloured card
- Scissors
- Ruler
- PVA glue or glue stick

Make the building blocks

The first step is to turn flat card into shapes that you can build with. For a construction like this, you will need 18 hexagonal prisms, 11 hexagonal pyramids and 7 cuboids.

1 Trace the net templates on page 196.

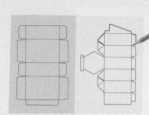

2 Copy the nets onto your chosen colour of card and cut them out.

3 Ask an adult to score along all the fold lines using a ruler and scissors.

4 Fold each scored line over. To get a neat edge, run a ruler along the fold.

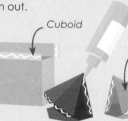

Cuboid

Hexagonal prism

Hexagonal pyramid

5 Glue the tabs to the inside of the main body of all the nets to make your 3D shapes.

This tower is made from stacked cuboids.

DID YOU KNOW?

Cinderella's castle inspired the castles at Walt Disney World's Magic Kingdom in Florida, USA and at Tokyo Disneyland in Japan.

The tallest tower has a gold roof.

Construct your castle

Once you have all your blocks, you can stack and glue them together to make towers and the outer wall, and bring your castle to life.

You can vary the height of your towers.

1 Stack prisms or cuboids to make castle towers. Top them all with pyramids and glue them together.

2 Glue pyramids on prisms for the low outer-wall towers.

3 Cut out crenellated strips of gold card.

4 Glue the strips around the top of each tower and along the cuboid wall pieces.

Lay the cuboids lengthways.

5 Glue the wall together, starting with a low tower, then alternating cuboids and towers.

6 Cut out a black semicircle of card and glue it to the central wall to make an archway.

7 Arrange the towers behind the wall.

Paper Planes

Ever dreamed of being a racing star like Dusty the crop-spraying plane did? Now you have the chance with these souped-up paper aeroplanes. Race with friends to see whose flies the furthest.

You will need:

- Tracing paper
- Pencil
- Coloured card
- Scissors
- Glue
- Paper clip
- Coloured paper, pens or paint

Skipper Riley

Skipper is an old Navy Corsair plane.

Assemble your plane

An ace pilot is only as good as their machine. First of all, build your plane to race with. Use the template but then decorate it to look like whichever plane is your favourite!

1 Trace the template on page 197.

2 Copy the two shapes onto card and cut them out.

3 Fold the larger card shape in half and then fold the wings out.

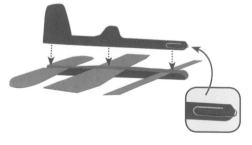

4 Glue the smaller piece of card inside the middle of the larger one.

5 Put a paper clip on the front end of the smaller card piece.

6 To seal the paper clip in place, wrap the thin strip at the end of the template around the plane's nose. Glue it in place.

7 Check how your plane flies. You might like to adjust the angle of the wings or tail.

8 Decorate your plane. You could use coloured paper, pens or paint. Now you're ready to fly!

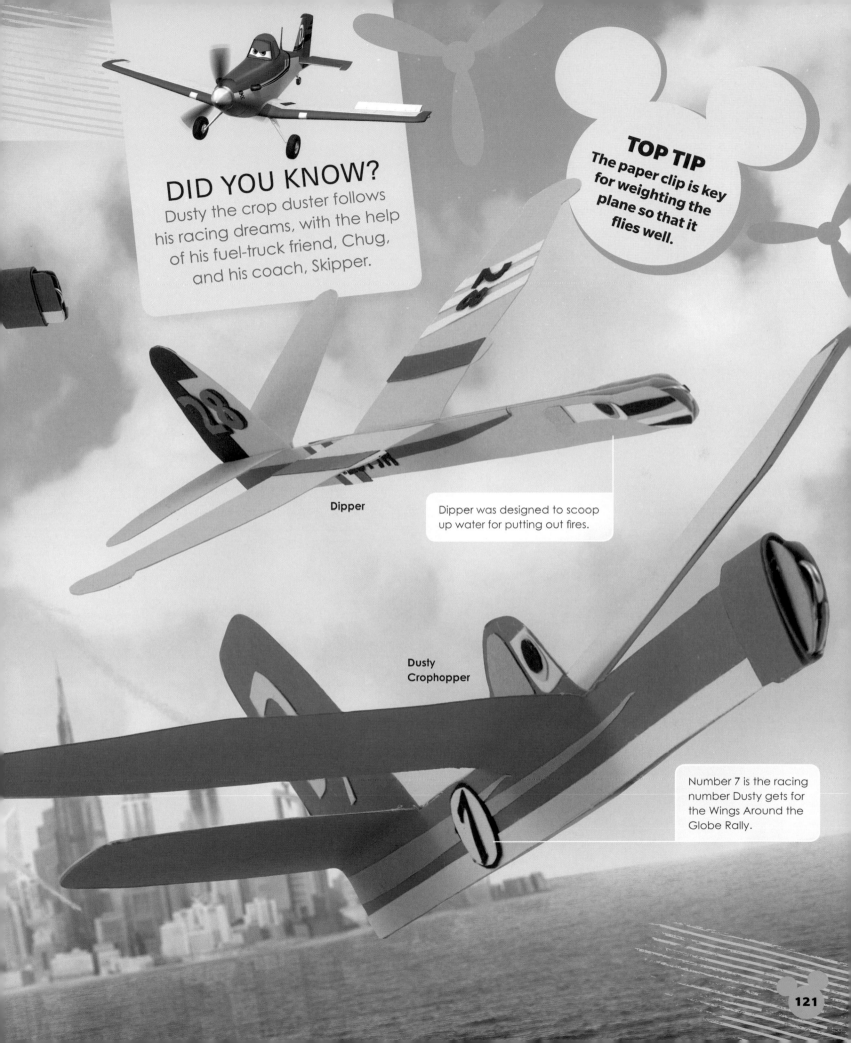

DID YOU KNOW?

Dusty the crop duster follows his racing dreams, with the help of his fuel-truck friend, Chug, and his coach, Skipper.

TOP TIP
The paper clip is key for weighting the plane so that it flies well.

Dipper

Dipper was designed to scoop up water for putting out fires.

Dusty Crophopper

Number 7 is the racing number Dusty gets for the Wings Around the Globe Rally.

ALADDIN

Shoebox Theatre

Conjure up a whole new world and some razzle-dazzle with this Aladdin-themed puppet show. Entertain your friends in a spectacular performance where you control what happens and can make wishes come true!

You will need:

- Shoebox
- Pencil
- Coloured card or paper
- Scissors
- PVA glue
- Paintbrush for glue
- Sticky tape
- Double-sided tape
- Ruler
- Craft knife
- Felt-tip pens
- Glue stick
- Sequins and glitter
- Gold fabric
- Wooden dowels

Build the stage

A shoebox is a perfect pre-made base for a puppet theatre. Transform yours by adding the Cave of Wonders' tiger-face front.

Orange paper for sand inside the cave

1 Remove the lid from your shoebox and cover the box part in coloured card.

2 Line the inside of the box with a different-coloured card or paper.

3 Draw four straight lines with a ruler on the top of the box.

4 Ask an adult to cut slits along the lines with a craft knife. They need to be wider than the wooden dowels.

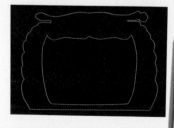

5 Draw the shape of the cave's tiger face and giant mouth on coloured card. Cut it out.

6 Cut out eyes, nose, and teeth from card, and glue or tape them on.

Set the scene

Shiny gold fabric, sequins and glitter create the sparkling Cave of Wonders, which is bursting with treasures.

Mounds of treasure   *Golden gate*

1 Make the scenery by drawing shapes on coloured card and cutting them out. Include a tab at the bottom of each piece.

2 Spread PVA glue on one side of the mounds of treasure, and add sequins and glitter on top.

3 Fold over the card tabs and glue them to the stage floor. Make sure everything is placed in between (not directly below) the slits in the top of the box.

Glitter and sequins look like gold treasure and sparkling jewels.

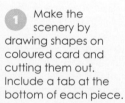 

4 Glue glitter to the floor of the stage and scatter gold sequins.

5 Cut gold fabric to make two curtains. Attach one on either side of the stage with double-sided tape.

6 Attach the tiger's face to the front of the stage with double-sided tape.

DID YOU KNOW?
The Cave of Wonders is hidden beneath the Arabian desert. It's here that Aladdin meets the Magic Carpet and finds the lamp with its powerful Genie.

TOP TIP
Place your characters at different heights on the dowels for a more interesting composition on the stage.

Tiger's head hides the edges of the shoebox.

Puppets are staggered to create a 3D effect on stage.

Make the puppets
The puppets are controlled from above with wooden dowels. Each one can be inserted through one of the slits you made in the top of the box.

Make your characters wide enough to tape the dowels behind.

Thick card will make your puppets strong and prevent damage when they're moved in and out of the slots.

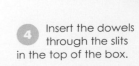

1. Draw the characters on card and cut them out.

2. Add details to the characters with coloured card or felt-tip pens.

3. Tape a wooden dowel to the back of each character.

4. Insert the dowels through the slits in the top of the box.

Set the shoebox scene
Put on your own Aladdin puppet show, using the sticks to move the characters around. You could even put on voices for each of the characters and tell the movie story – or make up your own tale!

Levitation Trick

TOP TIP
Try drawing different objects to amaze and astound your friends.

Princess Elena lives in a world full of magic. She gained special powers after being trapped in the Amulet of Avalor. Try your hand at making your own magic with this clever trick.

You will need:

- Card
- Coloured pens or pencils
- Scissors
- Sticky tape or sticky tac
- Glitter or glitter pens (optional)

Prepare your prop

There are all sorts of magical objects in Avalor, but Elena's Scepter of Light is one of the oldest and most powerful.

1 Draw and colour a picture of Elena's Scepter on card.

2 You can add sparkly glitter to distract your audience during the trick, and also make the Scepter look more impressive.

3 Cut the card with the Scepter on it into a playing-card size and shape.

Trying out the trick

With your prop ready, it's time to make things fly! However, as with all magic tricks, it is better to practise before you perform.

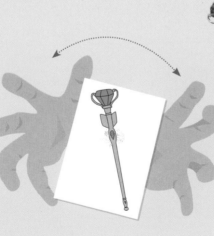

1 Place a small piece of tape or sticky tac on the tip of one of your thumbs. Press your thumb onto the back of the Scepter card.

2 Hold up the Scepter between your hands, moving them with magical flourishes. If you spread out your hands and fingers, it will look like the Scepter is floating in mid-air!

DID YOU KNOW?

Elena's wizard friend, Mateo, also has magical powers. He perform spells by striking his tamborita (drum wand).

Constellation Jar

When Hercules proves himself a true hero, his father, Zeus, hangs a picture of him in the stars. You can see the constellation (group of stars), named Hercules, in our sky. Make your own version for stargazing at home!

You will need:

- Clear jar or container
- Black paper or card
- Pencil
- Scissors
- Sticky tac
- Double-sided tape
- A flat torch or battery tealight that fits inside your jar

Star maker

You can draw any starry pattern you like, but it's important to make sure your black card fits the jar tightly so that light can only escape through the constellation.

1 Place your jar on card or paper, and mark how long and wide it needs to be to wrap around your jar. Cut it out.

2 Draw your constellation in the centre of the paper.

3 Push a pencil through the paper, into sticky tac, to make a hole for each star. You could also use a hole punch.

4 You could join up the stars in your constellation by cutting thin lines in the paper. This will highlight your pattern.

5 Tape the paper around the jar, making sure there are no gaps.

6 Turn off the lights. Turn on your light source, put it on its side in the jar, and replace the lid. Point the jar at a plain wall – and let the stargazing begin!

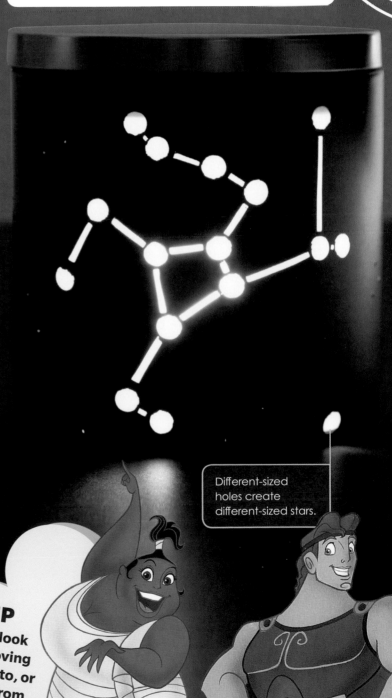

Different-sized holes create different-sized stars.

TOP TIP
If your stars look blurry, try moving your jar closer to, or further away from, your wall.

Belle's Book Garland

Belle always has her nose in a book. She is delighted with the Beast's library – a lifetime's worth of reading all in one room. Like Belle, you can surround yourself with books with this beautiful garland.

You will need:

- Decorated paper
- Coloured paper
- Plain white paper
- Pencil and ruler
- Scissors
- Glue stick
- Gold ribbon
- Sticky tape
- String
- Gold cord

Perfect the binding

Each book has a patterned outside cover and a coloured inside cover, with white interior pages. You could use wrapping paper for the outer covers, or create your own design.

1 To save time, you could cut all the different types of paper in advance. Rectangles 12.5 x 20 cm (5 x 7½ in) make good-sized books.

2 Glue a patterned piece of paper back-to-back with a coloured piece to make a book cover.

3 Fold the book cover in half so that the patterned side is on the outside.

Messages can be written on the inside white pages.

DID YOU KNOW?

Belle's favourite book is about a girl who meets "le Prince Charmant", which means Prince Charming in French.

4 Cut a 2.5 cm (1 in) piece of gold ribbon. This will become the tab to hang your book from.

5 Fold the ribbon in half to make a loop and tape the ends inside the top of the book.

6 Fold at least two pieces of white paper in half, so that they neatly fit inside your book cover.

7 Place the folded pieces of paper inside the cover.

8 Place a piece of string around the fold of the whole book.

9 Tie the string at the bottom so it holds everything together.

10 Repeat steps 2 to 9 to make as many books as you like. Then thread the gold cord through the loops.

11 Now it's time to hang up your garland!

Ribbon loops around the cord.

You could use a different pattern for every book.

Will o' the Wisps

Tiny, glowing creatures called will o' the wisps guide Princess Merida through the dark hills of the Scottish Highlands. You can create the same floating light effect with glow sticks. Where will your wisps lead you?

Make your own wisps

You can prepare the bottles in advance and then add the glow sticks just before you want the wisps to glow in the dark.

You will need:

- Plastic bottles
- Scissors
- Cotton wool
- PVA glue
- Blue glow sticks

Be careful of sharp edges!

1. Ask an adult to cut the top off the plastic bottle with scissors. One bottle will create one wisp.

Varying the thickness of cotton wool gives different shades of blue light.

2. Gently fluff and stretch pieces of cotton wool to make different shapes and thicknesses.

Several glow sticks in one bottle will strengthen the light.

3. Glue the pieces of cotton wool all around the outside of the bottle with PVA glue. Leave to dry.

4. Once the glue is dry, you can tease the cotton wool into different shapes to give the wisps character.

5. Crack glow sticks and put them in the bottle. Turn off the lights to watch your wisps glow. An average glow stick will last for one hour.

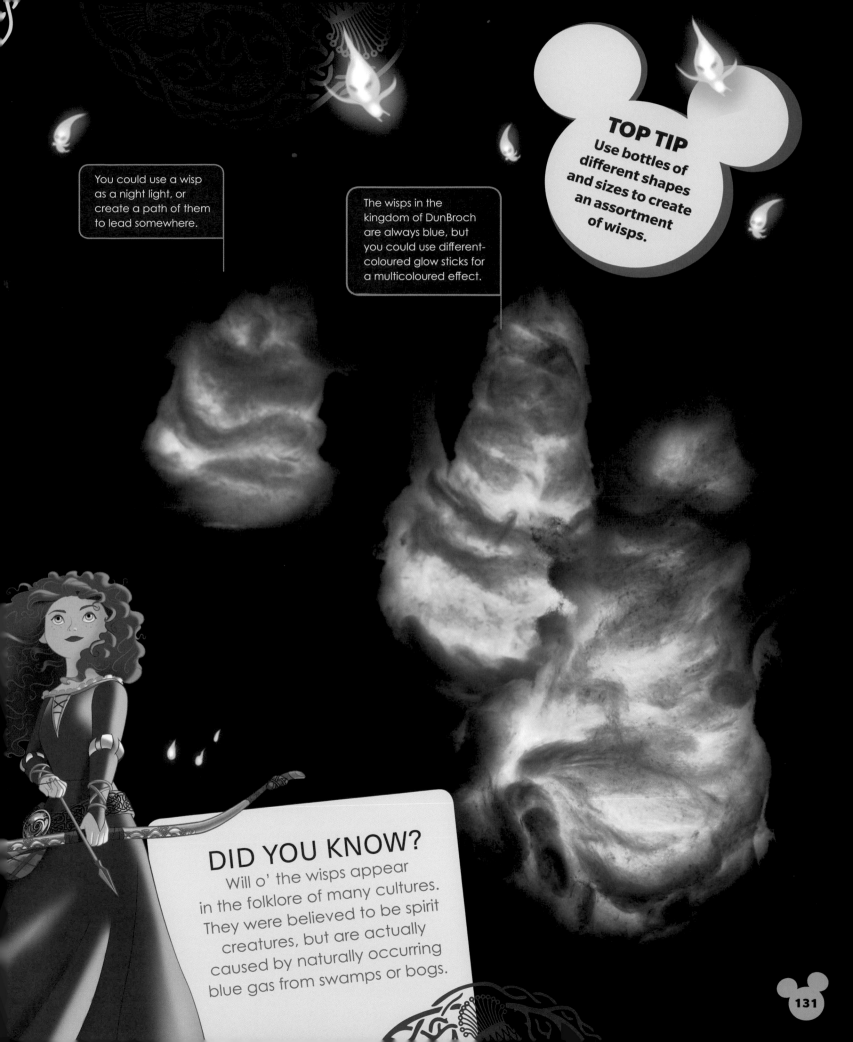

You could use a wisp as a night light, or create a path of them to lead somewhere.

The wisps in the kingdom of DunBroch are always blue, but you could use different-coloured glow sticks for a multicoloured effect.

TOP TIP
Use bottles of different shapes and sizes to create an assortment of wisps.

DID YOU KNOW?
Will o' the wisps appear in the folklore of many cultures. They were believed to be spirit creatures, but are actually caused by naturally occurring blue gas from swamps or bogs.

Zoetrope

Peter Pan visited Wendy, John and Michael in Victorian-era London. At this time, zoetropes were used to create animations. You can make one, too, and then watch Peter soar above the London skyline!

You will need:

- Paper plate
- Black card 10 cm (4 in) wide
- Scissors
- Coloured paper and card
- Felt-tip pens or paint
- Glue
- Sticky tape
- Pencil
- Sticky tac

Get prepared

A zoetrope is a cylinder with pictures that spins on a base. You can make a version of one with card and a paper plate.

1 Cut black card so it fits in a circle on your plate, with an extra 2.5 cm (1 in) for overlap.

2 At the top, cut slits 5 cm (2 in) long, spaced at regular intervals all the way along.

3 Along the bottom, cut away all but four evenly spaced tabs, 2.5 cm (1 in) long.

Draw your animation

Inside a zoetrope is a series of drawings that change slightly from one to the next. You could draw Peter Pan flying over London, or Neverland, or anything you like.

You could add famous buildings, or keep the shapes simple.

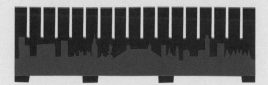

1 For an interior sky scene, cut a strip of light-blue paper the length of the black card and half as high.

2 Draw an image at regular intervals all the way around. It should vary slightly each time.

3 On coloured card, draw and cut out a cityscape or scene of your choice.

4 Glue the cityscape around the outside of the black card.

5 Glue the interior scene inside the black card.

Make sure the paper sits between the tabs, below, and slits, above.

Bring it together

As the zoetrope spins, your eyes see the pictures appear and disappear through the slits. This makes them look like they're one picture that's moving.

TOP TIP
Make sure that the images you repeat (such as Peter Pan) are all the same size.

Remember to stick the cityscape onto the outside!

1 Glue or tape the edges of the black card together to make a cylinder.

2 Bend over the tabs and glue them to the plate.

3 Attach the end of a pencil to the centre of the underside of the plate with sticky tac.

4 Twist the pencil between your fingers to make the whole thing spin.

Make sure you look through the slits, otherwise the pictures will appear blurred.

DID YOU KNOW?
When you see the images quickly in turn, your brain fills in the gaps and sees movement. This is the same way flipbooks and televisions work.

Boogie with Baloo

Baloo is an upbeat bear who just loves to sing and dance. Let this big-hearted bear teach you everything he knows about dancing. Forget your troubles and strife – just dance!

You will need:

- Space to dance
- Music (optional)

DID YOU KNOW?
Baloo may be laid back, but he's very ticklish!

Baloo
Baloo is a big, friendly bear who takes Mowgli under his paw. He teaches his new friend about his philosophy of an easy life, and saves him from many of the dangers in the jungle.

TOP TIP
You don't need fancy steps to dance; just jump up and feel the rhythm.

The Hop
This cool step means you can give your feet a rest – but only one at a time!

The Funky Vulture
Wiggle your elbows and make like those wacky birds.

The Stomp
Bear down on the dance floor and stomp those paws!

The Towel Twist
This groovy move is just like towelling off after a swim.

The Tail Feather
Shake it, baby! Even if you haven't got a tail, it's wild to wiggle.

The Kung Fu Kick
Hey – Baloo's got a black belt in the art of boogie!

ALICE IN WONDERLAND
Teacup Races

TOP TIP
Play this at a birthday party or at an "un-birthday" party! The March Hare and the Mad Hatter would.

Down the Rabbit Hole, Alice meets the March Hare and the Mad Hatter, who are a strange pair. Combine their love of tea and crazy capers in this Wonderland-themed race.

You will need:

- An outside space
- A plastic cup for each player
- Water

HOW TO PLAY:

1. All players need a cup full of water. Make sure everyone has an equal amount.

2. Everyone lines up at the starting line.

3. The referee shouts "Go" or blows a whistle. All racers make their way to the finishing line as quickly as possible without spilling their water.

4. The winner can be whoever is first over the line, whoever has the most water left or a combination of the two.

DISNEY
Sing-Off

Disney characters always break into the perfect song for any moment. Challenge your friends to find a Disney song for certain categories in this singing contest.

You will need:

- Knowledge of Disney songs

HOW TO PLAY:

1. Choose a theme, such as love or friendship.

2. Each team or person has to think of a song related to the theme. Make the game more difficult by picking specific words that songs must have in them.

3. Keep going until someone can't think of another song in your chosen theme. That person is out!

4. The others move on to the next round, with a different theme. The winner is the last person left.

Pixie-Dust Lip Gloss

Tiny Tinker Bell is a fairy who radiates a magic glow. A trail of pixie dust twinkles after her when she flies. Use some sparkle to make glittery lip gloss so you can shine just like Tink.

You will need:

- Petroleum jelly
- Food colouring
- Microwave
- Microwave-safe bowl
- Spoon
- Edible glitter
- Small jar
- Ribbon (optional)

Get prepared

Petroleum jelly is usually used for protecting skin, but you're giving it a much more fun purpose!

1 Place the petroleum jelly in a microwave-safe bowl. For one jar, you will need 30 ml (5 tsp) jelly.

2 Ask an adult to help you slowly soften the petroleum jelly in the microwave. Warm it up in 30-second bursts, stirring in between.

Mix it up

Now is the time to add a little magic to your lip gloss with a sprinkle of pixie dust.

1 Stir in a teaspoon of edible glitter. You can always add more if you want extra sparkle.

2 Add food colouring in small amounts until you get the shade you want.

3 Pour or spoon the mixture into your jar. Lightly tap the jar to get rid of air bubbles.

4 If the mixture is not smooth on top, ask an adult to warm the jar up in a bowl over a saucepan of boiling water.

5 Let the mixture cool before you apply it or put on the lid.

6 Decorate the jar with ribbon.

DID YOU KNOW?

Tinker Bell is a pots-and-pans fairy. She is great at mending things.

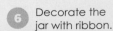

TOP TIP
If you want to make lip gloss in different colours, separate your mixture into different containers before stirring in food colouring.

Gold glitter represents golden pixie dust.

Red colouring for Rosetta, a garden-talent fairy

Glow-in-the-Dark Stars

King Mufasa tells his son, Simba, that the great kings of the past look down on them from the stars. Craft these stars to put on your ceiling to remind you of the people and things that are important to you.

You will need:

- Glow-in-the-dark polymer clay
- Cling film
- Rolling pin
- Cookie cutters
- Baking tray
- Oven
- Sticky tac

Shape and bake

Stars made from glow-in-the-dark clay will shine just like real stars in the night sky.

1. Pre-heat the oven, following the clay package instructions.

2. Roll out the clay until it is even and ½ cm (¼ in) thick.

3. Cut out star shapes with the cookie cutters.

4. Place the stars on a baking tray.

5. Bake in the oven for 30 minutes at 130°C (250°F) or according to the package instructions.

6. Once the stars have cooled, use sticky tac to arrange them on your ceiling.

Different-sized stars will create a sense of depth and distance.

You could shape your stars by hand or with a blunt knife.

TOP TIP
To keep the clay clean while you're rolling it out, lay a sheet of cling film on it.

Cola Volcano

Diet Cola Mountain stands tall in the video game *Sugar Rush*. When Ralph drops mints into its cola, it erupts in a blast of cola foam. You can recreate this dramatic explosion at home!

You will need:

- Full, unopened bottle of cola
- Paper
- Sugar-coated chewy mints

Foam shoots out of the bottle.

Make an explosion!

The key to ensuring a dramatic volcano is to start with a full, unopened bottle of cola. The cola will create a lot of mess, so it's best to do it outside. Make sure you have adult supervision.

1. Put your bottle in a safe place for setting off the explosion. Set it down carefully and let the cola settle.

2. Pour out about 60 ml (2fl oz) of the cola to make space in the top of the bottle.

3. Roll paper into a cylinder shape.

4. Place six mints in the cylinder of paper, holding your finger over the bottom to stop the mints falling out.

5. Unscrew the lid of the bottle.

6. Hold the cylinder over the bottle while standing as far back as possible.

7. Drop the mints into the bottle, and move away. Then watch the explosion unfold! Adding more mints will create an even bigger, faster explosion.

You could build a papier-mâché base or scene for your Diet Cola Mountain volcano.

The land of *Sugar Rush* has chocolate hills with icing swirls!

DID YOU KNOW?

Dissolved carbon gas in the cola reacts with tiny pits on the surface of the mints, rapidly forming bubbles and foam that shoots out of the bottle.

Piston-Cup Racetrack

Can't get to the Piston Cup? Don't worry – build a racetrack and host your own championship! Ramp up the excitement with a cardboard slope and your own cars.

You will need:

- Thick cardboard
- Ruler
- Pencil
- Scissors
- Sticky tape
- Glue
- Paint and paintbrush
- White and coloured paper
- Felt-tip pens
- Toothpicks
- Small toy cars

Prepare your pieces

Cut out all the pieces you will need, so when it's time to put your racetrack together, you'll be ready to get set, go!

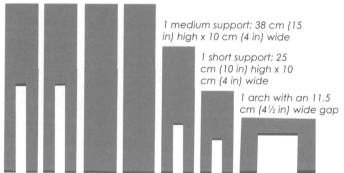

4 tall tower supports: 50 cm (20 in) high x 10 cm (4 in) wide

1 medium support: 38 cm (15 in) high x 10 cm (4 in) wide

1 short support: 25 cm (10 in) high x 10 cm (4 in) wide

1 arch with an 11.5 cm (4½ in) wide gap

Track piece A: 125 cm (50 in) long x 15 cm (6 in) wide

Pencil marks

Track piece B: 62.5 cm (25 in) long x 15 cm (6 in) wide

Platform piece: 20 cm (8 in) wide

Divider piece C: 125 cm (50 in) long x 5 cm (2 in) wide

Divider piece D: 25 cm (10 in) long x 5 cm (2 in) wide

1 Cutting thick cardboard can be hard work, so get an adult to help cut all the shapes.

2 On track pieces A and B, measure 2.5 cm (1 in) from the two long edges and from one short edge. Mark the lines with a pencil.

3 Cut out two square corners on piece A, as shown. This will allow the two track pieces to join together smoothly.

4 Measure 2.5 cm (1 in) from the edge of each side of the platform piece and mark the lines with a pencil. This will become the platform.

Make the ramp

The length and the height of your ramp will determine how steep the slope will be. A divider runs down the middle to separate the lanes.

The tab sits above the join on the top-side of the track.

Wall stops cars zooming off the track!

1 Tape together the short ends of pieces A and B on the underside to make one long track.

2 Ask an adult to score along the pencil lines with a ruler and a pair of scissors.

3 Fold the sides up to make track walls.

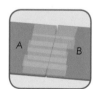

Finish line will be here.

C

A

B

D

4 At the scored end of piece B, cut slits and stick the folded-up corners together to make the end of the track.

5 Tape divider piece C in the centre of track piece A. This will run the length of the track's slope.

6 Tape divider piece D in the middle of track piece B, so it starts from the end of divider piece C.

Race to the finish!

Time to assemble the ramp and supports, then decorate your creation!

1 Tape together the four tall supports to make a tower.

 2 Ask an adult to score the platform pencil lines with a ruler and scissors.

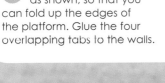

3 Cut a slit in each corner as shown, so that you can fold up the edges of the platform. Glue the four overlapping tabs to the walls.

Tab is stuck to the platform wall.

4 Cut a gap in the centre of one platform wall and fold the cardboard out, so the cars can access the track.

5 Tape the ramp to the top of the tower.

6 Tape the platform on top of the tower, with the gap lining up to the track.

7 Tape the two shorter supports below the track and the arch above the track.

8 Paint all your pieces and add a chequered strip on the track for a finish line.

9 Add signs at the start and finish lines by inserting toothpicks into the cardboard edges.

10 Add extra flags in the same way.

You can cut decorative archways in four of the supports.

FINISH

TOP TIP
This track fits cars smaller than 5 cm (2 in) wide. Adjust the size of your track if your vehicles are bigger.

DID YOU KNOW?
Lightning McQueen has won seven Piston Cup races.

Raft Building

Does the ocean call to you? Take to the water like Moana with this raft project that combines science, technology, engineering and maths. See how far you'll go with the wind in your sail!

You will need:

- Approximately 14 thin, straight twigs
- Wool
- Scissors
- Sticky tape
- Plain fabric
- Pencil
- Fabric pen
- Darning needle
- Strong glue

Make a raft

You'll need about 10 thin, straight twigs for the base. If they're not the same length, ask an adult to trim them for you. You'll also need two twigs for the sail and two shorter ones to cross the raft.

1 Tie a piece of wool around the end of one twig.

2 Wind it around a second twig, making a figure-eight loop. Repeat this back and forward a few times until it feels secure.

3 Repeat the same pattern from the second to a third twig and on until all 10 twigs are connected together.

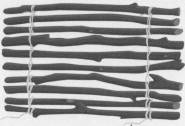

Tie off and trim your loose ends.

This twig should be long enough to lie across your raft.

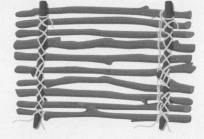

4 Tie a tight knot after the tenth twig and trim the excess yarn. Repeat this process for the other side of the raft, so both edges are secured.

5 Tie wool around one end of a shorter twig.

6 With the raft lying sideways, place the twig vertically across one end. Thread the wool around the twig, weaving it in and out of the twigs underneath.

7 Follow the same process with a new twig at the other end of the raft.

TRY THIS!
To keep the twigs still while you weave, you could temporarily stick them to a table with sticky tape.

Add a sail

You can't sail a boat without a sail! Moana's is decorated with the red, swirling symbol that was on the heart of Te Fiti.

A triangle-shaped sail catches the wind well and makes boats sail fast.

1 Lay the stick that will make the mast on a piece of fabric. Add a shorter twig at an angle that you like.

2 Draw between the twigs to make a triangular sail on the fabric. Cut it out.

3 Using a fabric pen, draw Moana's swirling symbol on the sail.

4 Wind red wool around the two twigs to join them together in a figure-of-eight loop, as above.

To draw on the sail, use a fabric pen so the pattern won't run if your raft overturns!

This raft is 10 twigs wide.

The supporting twigs running across your raft help it to float. They can sit on the top or underneath.

DID YOU KNOW?
Moana sails a single-hulled outrigger canoe – a wooden sailing boat that she finds in the cavern of her ancestors.

5 Make holes along the right-hand edge of the sail with a darning needle. Thread the red wool through the holes in the sail and around the mast.

6 Secure the wool at the top of the mast with a tight knot. Trim off the end.

7 Glue the bottom edge of the sail to the shorter twig.

8 Slot the mast in between twigs in the raft. Natural bends in the wood should allow this.

9 To secure the mast, wrap wool around its base, the twigs in the raft and the twig running across.

Clothes Peg Mermaids

Princess Ariel, from the kingdom of Atlantica under the sea, loves collecting curious human objects, including forks and combs. In this activity, collect spare clothes pegs and make playable dolls of Ariel and her mermaid sisters.

You will need:

- Straight wooden clothes pegs
- Pencil
- Acrylic paint
- Fine paintbrush
- Craft foam
- Scissors
- Glue
- Embroidery thread
- Glitter

Arista

Aquata

You could use coloured paper to create a pretty, watery backdrop.

Make a mermaid

The colours of this mermaid are for Ariel, but you could make any of her sisters, or your own creation.

1 Lay the clothes peg down with the rounded end at the top for a head.

2 Decide how far up the tail will come, draw a "V" shape, and paint everything below it.

3 Paint a seashell top. Ariel's tail is green, and her top is light purple.

4 Draw a tail shape on craft foam and cut it out.

5 Slot the foam tail inside the clothes peg. If needed, add glue or an extra wedge of foam to hold it in place.

6 Cut a length of thread long enough to wrap around the head three times. Glue it in place.

7 Cut 12 pieces of thread nearly twice the length of the clothes peg.

8 Bunch the 12 threads together, fold them in half and glue them to the top of the head.

9 Style the hair any way you like. You might need to add extra glue to the back of the head.

10 Paint a simple face, such as two eyes and a smile.

11 Once the paint and glue are dry, paint any extra details you like and add glitter for underwater sparkle.

Stick the hair behind the thread you added in step 6.

Ariel

DID YOU KNOW?

Ariel has six sisters named Aquata, Andrina, Arista, Attina, Adella and Alana.

TOP TIP

Mark out the clothes and the top of the tail in pencil before you add paint.

147

Paper Elephant Parade

Dumbo can't believe his eyes when he sees a parade of pink elephants. It seems unreal, but with a few clever techniques, you can transform plain paper into a marching band of elephants!

You will need:

- 7 sheets of coloured paper for each elephant
- White paper
- Pencil
- Glue
- Scissors
- Double-sided tape
- Googly eyes

Prepare your elephants

The first elephant step is to create all the body parts out of paper.

1 Glue all the way along one side of one of the coloured pieces of paper.

2 Curl the paper into a cylinder and stick down the opposite edge onto the glued edge.

3 Draw 12 toenails on the white paper, and cut them out.

4 Glue three toenails onto the bottom of the leg.

5 Repeat these steps so you have four tubes for legs.

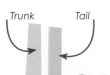

Trunk   Tail

6 Cut two long strips of coloured paper.

7 Tightly curl each strip around itself, then let go so it's loosely curled.

Bring your elephants to life

Once you've made all the pieces, stick them together, and you'll soon have an elephant in the room!

1 Place the four legs together and tape a whole sheet of paper over the top using double-sided tape. The edges of the top paper should fold over each side but not over the back. You may need to trim to fit.

2 Make a fifth cylinder and glue it horizontally onto the front of the body to make the head.

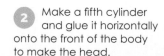

3 Glue the trunk to the middle of the head.

4 Stick the tail strip under the back of the elephant's body piece.

TOP TIP
Complete one elephant first so you know that you've got the right-sized pieces before you make a whole parade.

148

DID YOU KNOW?
Dumbo's real name is Jumbo Junior. He was given the nickname Dumbo by the other elephants in the circus.

5 Cut two ear shapes for each elephant.

7 Stick the googly eyes in place.

6 Tape or glue the ear pieces into each side of the head tube.

Instead of googly eyes, you could use paper dots or draw the eyes on with a pen.

Use smaller pieces of paper to make baby elephants as well as adults.

Hamm Piggy Bank

You can bank on Hamm to store your money safely. This cheery fellow is a piggy bank and one of Andy's toys. You can make your own Hamm from a plastic bottle to collect your coins in.

You will need:

- Empty plastic bottle with its lid
- Craft knife
- Tape
- Pen
- Cork stopper
- PVA glue
- Mixing container
- Newspaper
- Egg box
- Card
- Scissors
- Paint and paintbrush
- Strong glue
- Slotted button
- Pink pipe cleaner

Prepare your bottle

A fat bottle works best – a tapered one won't give you the right shape for Hamm's round face.

1 Ask an adult to cut the central section out of the bottle with a craft knife.

2 Tape the top and bottom of the bottle back together. This will make it shorter, rounder and more pig-shaped.

3 Draw around the cork on one side of the bottle.

Don't cover the holes you have made with newspaper.

4 Ask an adult to cut a hole for the cork and also a slot on the opposite side of the bottle.

5 Mix together equal amounts of PVA glue and water.

6 Tear up strips of newspaper and wet them with the glue mixture. Cover the bottle with the strips.

7 Once the papier mâché is dry, add another layer. You may need more than two layers.

Decorate your piggy bank

Once Hamm is covered with papier mâché and is completely dry, you can decorate him.

Dark-pink card ears

Card eyebrows

Card eyes

Egg-cup legs *Card toenails*

1 Cut out the egg cups and card shapes.

2 Paint the whole bottle, the four feet and the button light pink. Also paint the back and around the edges of the ears.

3 Once the paint is dry, attach the legs with a strong glue.

4 Fold over the edge of the ears and glue the flaps onto the bottle.

5 Glue on the eyes, eyebrows, button and toenails.

6 Put the cork in the hole.

7 Curl a pipe-cleaner tail and glue it on.

DID YOU KNOW?
Sometimes Andy plays a fantasy game where Hamm becomes a dastardly villain named Evil Dr Porkchop.

Make sure the slot is big enough to fit your coins through.

If the newspaper shows through, add another coat of paint.

Snowgie Snowflakes

Do you want to build a snowman? How about some smiley snowmen faces? These symmetrical snowflake designs are snowgies – the tiny, mischievous snowmen that appear when an unwell Elsa sneezes.

You will need:

- Tracing paper
- White paper
- Pencil
- Scissors
- Thin white thread
- Sticky tape
- Hole punch

TOP TIP
Keep the layers of folded paper tightly together while you're cutting.

Fold and cut

Each snowflake is made from just one sheet of plain white paper and a templated segment of a Snowgie. No sneezing required!

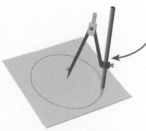

You could use a pair of compasses.

1 Draw a circle 12 cm (4¾ in) in diameter.

Make sure that your folds line up neatly.

2 Fold the circle into quarters, and then half again, with firm, straight creases.

3 Trace the template on page 197 onto the top segment of your circle.

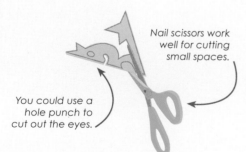

Nail scissors work well for cutting small spaces.

You could use a hole punch to cut out the eyes.

4 Carefully cut out the pattern. Because the paper is folded, you will cut through all parts at once.

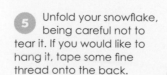

5 Unfold your snowflake, being careful not to tear it. If you would like to hang it, tape some fine thread onto the back.

DID YOU KNOW?

The snowgies all have names, including Slush, Sludge, Slide, Ansel, Flake, Fridge, Flurry and Powder!

This snowflake was folded into quarters, so it has four lines of symmetry.

For this design, the paper was folded in half and then into thirds, so it has six lines of symmetry.

Enchanted Rose Glitter Jar

Behold a beautiful enchanted rose! The Beast must find true love before the last petal falls. You can enjoy this glittering rose globe without being under a spell!

You will need:

- A jar with a lid
- Polymer clay (green and red)
- Modelling wire
- Baking tray
- Oven
- Strong glue
- Water
- Silk rose petals
- Glitter
- Glycerine

Build the stem

The Beast's rose floats in the air, but this one stands on a green clay stem strengthened with wire.

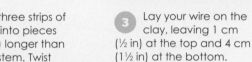

1 Make a flat rectangle shape with your green clay, smaller than the height of your jar.

2 Cut three strips of wire into pieces 5 cm (2 in) longer than your rose stem. Twist the wires together.

3 Lay your wire on the clay, leaving 1 cm (½ in) at the top and 4 cm (1½ in) at the bottom.

4 Wrap your clay around the wire, moulding it smooth with your fingers.

5 Bend your stem into an "S" shape to look like a real flower stem.

6 Make leaf shapes from green clay and attach them to the stem. You could add a vein detail with a fingernail.

7 Separate the bottom wire into three to help the stem stand up.

Grow the rose

A beautiful rose is easy to make; just wrap seven clay petals around each other.

1 Make petal shapes from the red clay.

2 Roll one petal in on itself to form the centre of the rose.

3 Wrap six petals around the centre of the rose, bending the top edges of the outer petals outwards.

4 Stick more petals around the bottom of the stem to cover up the wire.

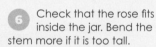

5 Push the rose head onto the wire and give it a little squeeze to make it secure.

6 Check that the rose fits inside the jar. Bend the stem more if it is too tall.

7 Place the rose on a baking tray.

8 Bake in the oven, following the clay package instructions.

9 Once cool, use strong glue to stick the rose onto the inside of the lid. Make sure you can still screw the lid on. Leave upright to dry.

Add magical sparkle

Once your glue is completely dry, it's time to add the finishing touches.

1 Fill the jar with water, almost to the top.

2 Add a teaspoon of glycerine. Too much might make your glitter clump together, while too little may make it fall too fast.

3 Add silk rose petals and a sprinkle of glitter.

4 Screw the lid on tightly.

5 Shake your jar, place it lid-down and watch the petals fall.

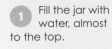
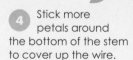

DID YOU KNOW?

An Enchantress's spell turned the Prince into a Beast and bewitched his castle.

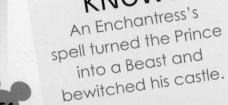

The rose was offered to the Prince by the Enchantress in exchange for shelter in his castle.

Glycerine in the jar makes the glitter fall gently.

Glitter sparkles when the jar is shaken.

Decorate the lid with coiled ribbon or cord.

TOP TIP
Seal the lid with glue around the outside of the jar, to stop any leaks.

Covered Notebooks

If you judge a book by its cover, you'll love these character-themed notebooks! You could make a set featuring Donald, Minnie and all their friends. Keep the whole collection for yourself or give them as gifts.

You will need:

- Coloured paper
- White paper
- Notebooks
- Pencil
- Scissors
- Double-sided tape or glue
- White buttons

Cover your notebook

Follow these steps for making Donald Duck, adapting the method for any other character or design you wish.

1 Choose the main colour for your notebook – for example, blue for Donald Duck's sailor shirt.

2 Place the notebook in the middle of the coloured paper. Open it out. You will need enough paper to cover the whole book: front, back and spine.

Draw around your book to mark its size.

3 Cut out the paper so it's 2.5 cm (1 in) larger than the book in all directions.

4 Cut triangles off all the corners. Measure against the notebook so that you don't cut deeper than the size of the book.

5 Cut out a small rectangle at the top and bottom of the spine, as shown.

6 Wrap the paper around the book. Fold the flaps inside the book's cover and stick them down with glue or double-sided tape.

7 Cut two strips of yellow paper and stick them in a "V" shape to make Donald's collar.

8 Cut out a bow tie from red paper and stick it to the point of the yellow "V" shape.

9 Glue four large white buttons below the bow tie to finish Donald's classic sailor look.

DID YOU KNOW?

In 2005, Donald Duck received his own star on the Hollywood Walk of Fame – a series of decorative stars built into pavements in Los Angeles, California, USA.

TOP TIP
You can add texture by using different materials for the accessories. How about a silky bow for Minnie?

To make Minnie

By using a different-coloured base paper, you can make any character. Here's how to create Minnie Mouse.

1 Wrap your notebook with dark-pink paper, following steps 2 to 6 above.

2 Using a coin or other round template, draw out lots of identical circles on white paper. Cut them out.

3 Glue your white circles on the light-pink paper. You could arrange them in a pattern or randomly.

4 Wrap the light-pink, polka-dot paper around the bottom half of your notebook.

157

Heroic Bookends

The Incredibles are Supers: upstanding members of society who look out for others. Get help from this super-powered family to keep your shelves in order. Elastigirl will stretch to make room for any number of books!

You will need:

- Tracing paper
- Pencil and pens
- Coloured card
- Glue or double-sided tape
- Scissors
- At least two mini cereal boxes
- Paper
- Uncooked rice

Make your characters

Create super-mum Elastigirl from card to guard your books. You can add her family using the same technique.

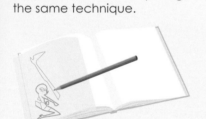

1 Copy the Elastigirl template on page 198 onto tracing paper.

2 Copy the main shape, including the separate leg piece, onto black card and cut it out.

3 Use your template to draw face and body details on red card.

Elastigirl

You could add other heroes or even villains.

Mr Incredible

4 Stick the details on to the figure with glue or double-sided tape.

5 For a minimalist look, draw on facial features with a white pen or pencil.

Build your bookends
To make the bookends heavy enough to support books, you need a base weighted down with rice.

1 Fill your mini cereal boxes with uncooked rice.

2 Wrap each mini cereal box. You could use patterned paper, or use plain paper and decorate it yourself.

3 Stick Elastigirl onto the boxes with glue.

TRY THIS!
You could paint the boxes instead of wrapping them, but you may need several coats of paint.

Decorate your boxes to look like a high-rise cityscape background.

Jack-Jack

DID YOU KNOW?
Elastigirl and Mr Incredible are in fact the married couple Helen and Bob Parr. They and their three children, Violet, Dash and baby Jack-Jack, all have awesome super powers.

Painted Eggs

"Off with their heads!" cries the Queen of Hearts whenever anyone displeases her. You can get your own back in this craft that creates an egg-head version of the fierce Queen. Here, you're the one in charge. Get cracking!

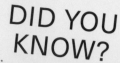

You will need:

- Raw egg
- Needle
- Drinking straw
- Small bowl
- Egg cup or small container
- Acrylic paint
- Black pen
- Yellow paper
- Scissors
- Sticky tape
- White paper doily
- Glue

If you don't have a paper doily, you can cut or decorate paper to make the collar.

Prepare your egg

The inside of an egg will go bad very quickly. This technique blows out the contents of the egg without damaging the shell too much.

1 Poke a needle through both ends of the egg.

2 With the needle, make one of the holes bigger until a straw will fit through it.

3 Gently blow through the straw.

4 Catch the contents of the egg in a bowl as it comes out of the smaller hole.

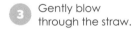

5 Once the shell is empty, run water very gently through it to wash it out.

6 Leave the eggshell to dry.

Decorate your egg

Once your egg is cleaned out and completely dry, it's ready for decorating.

1 For this stage, place your egg in a container, with the larger of the egg's holes at the bottom.

2 Paint the Queen's hair, earrings, eyes, nose and mouth. For the finer details, you could use a pen.

3 Cut zig-zags on a strip of paper to make a crown.

4 Tape the ends of the paper together. Attach the crown to the egg with sticky tape tabs.

5 Cut a paper doily with curved edges to make a frilly collar for the Queen.

6 Glue the collar around the Queen's neck. Her Eggcellency is now complete!

TRY THIS!
Make Tweedledum and Tweedledee, too! Use the smaller pin hole for adding paper flags.

Paper-Clip Friends

DID YOU KNOW?
Donald Duck has a twin sister named Della.

Cheerful stationery makes paperwork much more fun! Who better to decorate your desk than Mickey and his friends? With simple buttons, you can make some very familiar faces.

You will need:

- Buttons
- Felt
- Craft glue
- Scissors
- Colourful paper clips

Build faces out of buttons

Basic shapes can be combined for a powerful effect. Use round buttons as a base and then build up with more unusual shapes, or designs cut from felt.

Find buttons that look like eyes, a mouth or a beak!

1 Arrange your buttons on a piece of felt in the shape of your chosen character.

2 Glue your buttons onto the felt.

3 Cut extra felt shapes for details such as a bow tie and glue them onto the buttons.

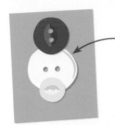

Mickey Mouse

Duffle-coat buttons are a good shape for long dog ears.

Goofy

Donald Duck

Tab

4 Cut out the whole shape, leaving a tab of felt under the head.

5 Push the tab under the top of a paper clip and glue to the back.

Minnie Mouse

Pluto

Daisy Duck

Party Straws

Drinking straws make a great nose for Pinocchio, whose nose gets longer each time he tells a lie. You can tell everyone that you made these fun straw toppers all by yourself – unless that's a lie, of course!

Decorate the straws

This simple craft instantly transforms ordinary straws.

Face Hat Hair Feather

Collar and hat band

1 Sketch out Pinocchio's face to work out the shapes and colours you will need.

2 Cut the shapes out and glue them onto card.

You will need:

- Pencil
- White card
- Coloured paper or card
- Scissors
- Glue stick
- Black pen
- Sticky tac
- Bendy drinking straws (reusable are best)

Feather piece sits under blue band.

3 Draw the eyes and the mouth with a black pen.

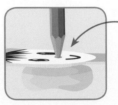

This makes a hole for the straw.

4 Ask an adult to push a sharp pencil through the card into sticky tac.

5 Now slide the face onto a straw. How long will you make his nose?

WINNIE THE POOH

Party Hats

No celebration in the Hundred-Acre Wood is complete without balloons, a pot of honey and, of course, party hats! Make these cheerful hats for your friends and let the fun begin.

You will need:

- Tracing paper
- Pencil
- Coloured card
- Scissors
- Glue or sticky tape
- A hole punch
- Thin elastic thread

Make Winnie the Pooh

Follow these steps to make the Winnie the Pooh hat, or adapt the process for other characters.

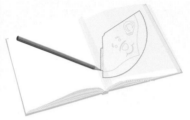

1 Trace the templates on page 199.

2 Copy the cone template onto yellow card and cut it out.

Use strips of pink paper for Piglet's body.

Winnie the Pooh

Piglet

3 Roll the card up into a cone.

Tab tucks inside the cone to help hold the hat together.

4 Stick the tab to the inside of the cone with glue or sticky tape.

5 Copy the ear shapes onto yellow card and carefully cut them out.

6 Copy the ear details onto white card, cut them out and stick them to the ears.

7 Fold over the tabs on the ears and stick them to the cone.

8 Copy the shape of Pooh's t-shirt onto red card and cut it out.

9 Stick the red strip around the bottom of the hat, with the thinner section at the front.

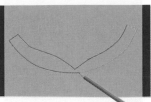

TOP TIP
Capture your character by including distinctive elements, such as Piglet's big ears or Tigger's stripes.

Plan out Tigger's face on scrap paper before you start.

Tigger

10 Copy the nose, eyes, mouth and other facial features onto black card. Cut them out and stick them onto the hat. If you prefer, you could draw all these details instead.

11 Use a hole punch to make a hole on either side of the face, near the bottom of the hat.

12 Measure a length of elastic that will fit comfortably under your chin and reach from hole to hole.

13 Thread the elastic through both holes and tie a knot in each end to secure it.

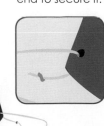

DID YOU KNOW?
Winnie the Pooh lives in the Hundred-Acre Wood along with his friends, who include Piglet, Tigger, Rabbit, Eeyore, Owl, Kanga and Roo.

Party Bags

The colourful *Toy Story* characters will brighten up any party table. These bags are all made with the same simple technique – just adapt the colours and shapes to make your favourite toys.

Decorate the bags

These bags can hold your party food or can be filled with treats for your guests to take home. Here are the steps for an Alien party bag.

Trace around your bag to get the right shape.

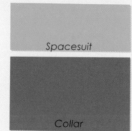

Spacesuit

Collar

Antenna

Mouth

Three eyes

Fold over the top one-third of the bag.

Mouth extends over the edge of the bag.

1 Draw the face you're going to make on paper to work out which shapes you'll need.

2 Draw all the pieces on thin coloured card and then carefully cut them out.

3 Draw pupils on the eyes with a black felt-tip pen.

4 Glue all the pieces onto the bag. The collar piece should be stuck before the spacesuit.

These bags would make great lunchbags, too!

TOP TIP
Try out your design on one bag before cutting out lots of faces. Then you can be sure your design will fit your bags.

Lots-o'-Huggin' Bear

Rex

A part of every face should hang over the fold.

Teeth details drawn with pen.

Alien

Hamm

You can add on extra features such as arms, eyebrows and ears.

Printed Gift Wrap

Make your mark on the gifts you give with this dino-tastic wrapping paper. Arlo the dinosaur and his family print their marks by dipping their feet in mud, but you can use paint for your own prehistoric printing.

Print a pattern

Using a templated shape to print from is an easy way to cover a large area with an identical, repeating pattern.

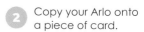

1 Using the template on page 197, trace the outline of Arlo.

2 Copy your Arlo onto a piece of card.

You will need:

- Card
- Scissors or craft knife
- Plain wrapping paper
- Poster paint
- Sponges (such as old kitchen sponges)

TOP TIP
Use matte, not shiny, wrapping paper so the paint sticks better. Brown paper also works well.

DID YOU KNOW?

Arlo the Apatosaurus befriends a little human whom he calls Spot.

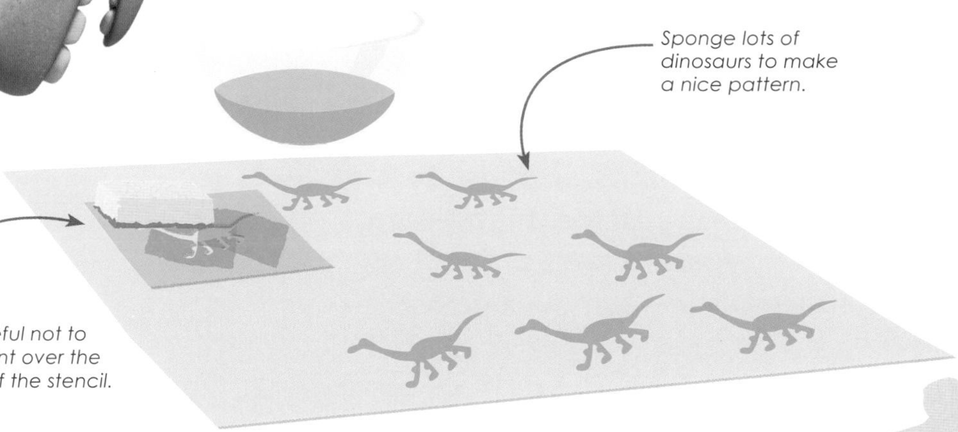

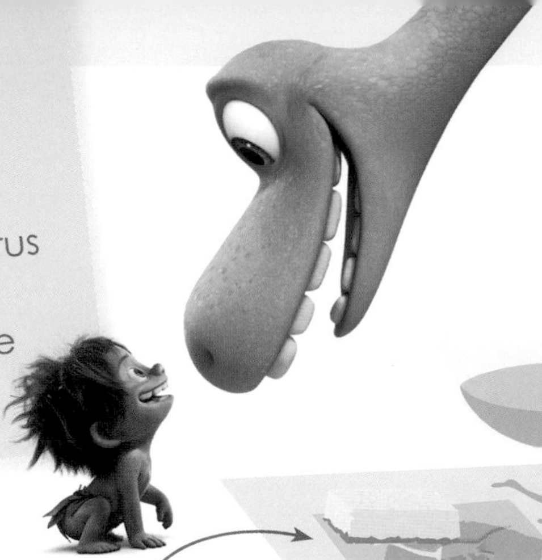

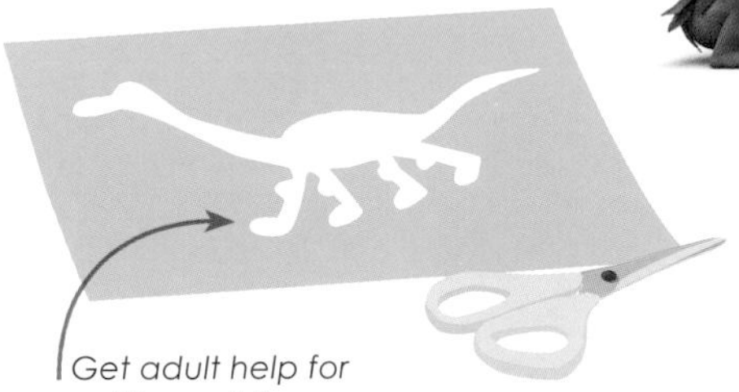

Get adult help for cutting out the finer details.

Be careful not to get paint over the edge of the stencil.

Sponge lots of dinosaurs to make a nice pattern.

3 Cut out inside the shape to make your stencil.

4 Place the stencil on the paper. Using a sponge, dab paint over the hole in the stencil. Repeat as many times as you like.

5 Wait for your paper to dry. Then wrap your presents!

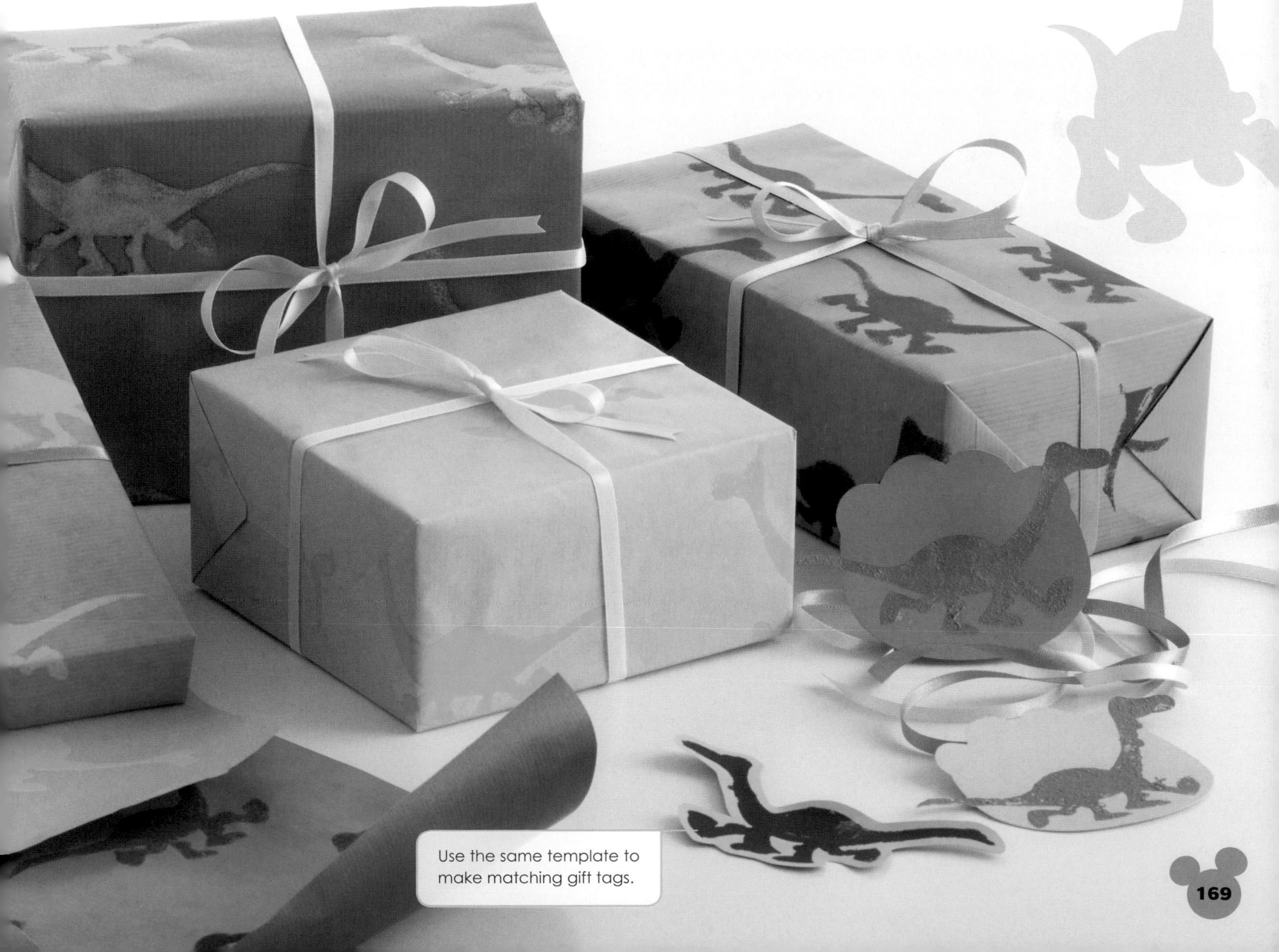

Use the same template to make matching gift tags.

Party Paper Chains

TOP TIP
For tidy chains, keep your paper strips the same length and overlap them the same amount.

Bring some Mickey and Minnie Mouse cheer to your room with these delightful paper chains. They're perfect for parties or even just for brightening things up. You never need an excuse to add some Disney to your decor!

You will need:

- Coloured paper
- Scissors
- Sticky tape
- Glue
- Small white dot stickers

You can change your designs to match Minnie's different colourful outfits.

Prepare the paper

A key difference between Mickey and Minnie is that Minnie wears a lot of polka dots. Prepare some paper for her dress fabric.

1 Cover pink paper in white dot stickers for Minnie's dress and bow.

Space the dots evenly in a repeating pattern.

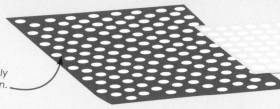

Assemble all the parts

Cut strips of paper for the decorative chains. You can make the chains as long as you like, depending on how many sets you cut.

1 For the Mickey chains, you need sets of:

Gloves

Tail

Use leftover black paper from the head pieces to make tails.

Mouse head with two ears

Red body with two dot stickers

Yellow feet

White strip

2 For the Minnie chains, you need sets of:

Mouse head with two ears

Spotty pink body

Plain pink feet

White strip

White strips add a space between each mouse.

You could use a ruler to make sure your paper strips are straight.

Gloves

Bow

Tail

DID YOU KNOW?

In early animations Mickey's ears always looked circular, whichever direction he faced.

Loop the chains together

Once you have all the parts you need, you can link them together in sets of four loops.

1 Fold the ears back so that they stick out from their strip.

2 Tape the ends of the head strip together to make a loop.

3 Thread the body strip over the bottom of the head loop and tape the ends together. Do the same with the feet strip and repeat until you have a chain.

4 Decorate the loops with the gloves, tails and bows.

5 You may need to rearrange your loops so the ears, gloves and tails line up.

Carrot Pen

Judy Hopps proves that even tiny bunnies can make excellent police officers. She succeeds thanks to her determination, her skill and her carrot-shaped pen that contains a recording device.

You will need:

- Air-drying clay
- Rolling pin
- Pen
- Water
- Pencil
- Ruler
- Acrylic paint

Shape your clay

Making an air-drying clay-cover for an ordinary pen can turn it into an extraordinary carrot pen.

1. Massage the clay with your hands to warm it up.

2. Mould your clay into a rough carrot shape.

3. Flatten the shape slightly with a rolling pin or your hands.

4. Place your pen on the clay so the point is just over the edge.

5. Wrap the clay around the pen and into the final carrot shape.

A little water can refresh dry clay.

6. Seal the clay using a dab of water along the seam.

Turn the pen into a carrot

A few simple additions and paint will transform your clay pen into a delicious-looking carrot.

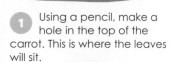

1. Using a pencil, make a hole in the top of the carrot. This is where the leaves will sit.

2. Make three leaf shapes with fresh clay. Mould them together at one end.

3. Shape a strip of clay to support the leaves.

4. Put the leaves into the hole in the carrot. Wrap the strip of clay around the leaves to hold them in place.

5. Use a ruler to score dents across the clay to create texture.

Scoring one oval makes it look like a speaker.

6. Roll out two small, flat clay ovals, one twice the length of the other.

7. Use water to stick each oval in the middle of the carrot, one on each side. Leave the clay to air-dry for 48 hours.

8. Once your carrot is completely dry, paint it orange and green.

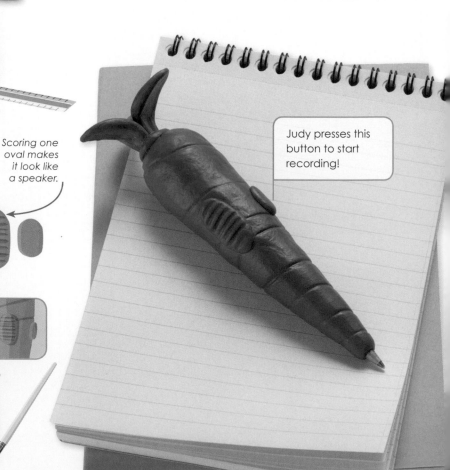

Judy presses this button to start recording!

Rapunzel Bookmark

Growing up imprisoned in a tower, Rapunzel learns about the outside world from books. Don't get in a tangle with your own reading. Use Rapunzel's long, golden hair to mark your place.

You will need:

- Tracing paper
- Pencil
- Colouring pencils, pens or paint
- White card
- Scissors
- Sticky tac
- Thin ribbon
- Sticky tape

Build the tower

The template on page 192 forms the main part of the bookmark. It's Rapunzel's tall tower, hidden deep in the forest.

1 Trace the template on page 192 onto tracing paper and then copy it onto card.

2 Colour in the tower – you could use pencils or paints – and cut it out.

> The top of Rapunzel's tower helps you find your page.

Let down Rapunzel's hair

Strands of Rapunzel's hair tumble out of the tower window, just as they will flow out of your book.

1 Place a small ball of sticky tac under the marked window.

2 Pierce a hole by pushing the pencil through the cards, into the sticky tac.

3 Cut three strands of ribbon 50 cm (20 in) long.

4 Thread the strands through the hole in the window and fasten with tape at the back.

5 Plait the strands all the way to the bottom.

6 Tie a knot in the base of the plait. Finish with a bow tied from pretty ribbon.

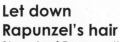

> Use yellow or gold ribbons for a hairlike plait.

Monster Pom-Poms

The monsters at Monsters University want to be tough, intimidating and scary. However, they (mostly) have good hearts, and sometimes the colourful furballs are just plain cute – especially when they're remade as pom-poms.

You will need:

- Stiff card
- Cups or pair of compasses
- Pencil
- Scissors
- Needle
- Coloured wool

Circle time

It's easy and fun to make your own pom-poms. Will yours be a monstrous size or teeny-tiny Mike-sized?

The larger the diameter of the whole circle, the bigger your pom-pom will be.

The thinner the ring, the bushier the pom-pom.

1 Draw two identical circles on the card 8 cm (3 in) wide. You could use a pair of compasses or draw around something round, such as the rim of a cup.

2 Draw a smaller circle inside each circle and cut out the inner circles, leaving two rings.

Wrap it up

You can make patterns or eyes on your pom-pom with different-coloured wool. Pom-poms are symmetrical, so any details you make on one half will repeat on the other. Follow these steps to make a Mike Wazowski pom-pom.

1 Place the two card rings on top of each other.

2 Wind black wool over one side of the rings, passing it through the hole as you go. Hold the first piece in place until the start of the wool is secure.

3 Keep going until you've wrapped it around about 20 times.

Keep all the black wool in a clump together.

4 Wrap a thin layer of blue wool on top of the black. Make the blue layer wider than the black on both sides.

5 Add white wool so it covers the blue in a thick layer, about 6 strands deep.

6 Wind green wool all over the ring. When a strand runs out, start a new piece from the outside edge of the ring.

When you finish with each colour, tuck in the end of the strand.

Try to keep your mound of wool even in shape and size so your final design will be even.

⚠ 7 When the central hole is too small to push wool through, use a needle to keep going until there is no hole left.

Unfurl your monster

Once your pom-pom has as much wool as it can take, it's time to open it up and reveal your fluffy monster.

1 Insert scissors between the two rings and cut the wool all the way around.

2 Cut a long piece of green wool and place it in between the rings, all the way around the pom-pom. Pull it as tightly as you can and knot. Wrap it around again, pull tightly and knot again.

This thread holds your pom-pom together.

Leave the strand long if you want to hang up your pom-pom.

3 Once your pom-pom is securely tied, pull or tear off the card rings.

4 Spread the wool out so your pom-pom is round and fluffy. Trim any long strands to make the pom-pom even.

Terri (left) and
Terry (right) Perry

Scattered wool
loops create
a spotty effect.

You can make
pom-poms with
two eyes, too.

Art

Add pipe cleaners
to bring your
pom-poms to life!

Mike Wazowski

James P. Sullivan
("Sulley")

DID YOU KNOW?
Monster Scarers spook children so they can collect their screams. They use them to power their world, as we use electricity.

Charm Bracelets

Disney Princesses express their personal style with their clothes and accessories. Use the princesses' special colours and symbols to make beautiful charm bracelets – or create your own designs.

You will need:

- Paper
- Pencil
- Shrink plastic
- Permanent markers
- Glitter pens (optional)
- Scissors
- Hole punch
- Oven
- Baking parchment
- Baking tray
- Jewellery links
- Pliers
- Ribbon in different colours

Make your charms

Shrink plastic designs become smaller when they're baked, but much thicker and bolder.

Don't use any oil-based or waxy crayons or paint. The ink will melt in the oven!

1 Design your charms on paper first.

2 Draw your designs on the shrink plastic with permanent markers or glitter pens. Charms work best with a diameter of around 7 cm (2¾ in).

Leave space to punch the hole!

3 Cut your charms out, leaving 0.5 cm (⅕ in) all the way around. Be careful of any sharp edges.

4 Work out which way up each charm should hang and punch a hole in the top of each one.

Bake your charms

Ask an adult to bake these charms for you. When they come out of the oven, they'll be hot, so don't touch them until they've cooled down!

1 Place the charms on baking parchment on a baking tray.

2 Ask an adult to bake the charms in a pre-heated oven at 160°C (320°F) for 2 minutes, but keep an eye on them.

3 Ask an adult to take the charms out of the oven and immediately press them under something flat and heavy, such as another baking tray with some books on top.

4 After the charms have had time to cool, ask an adult to add a jewellery link to each charm using pliers.

Cut the ribbons to lengths long enough to wrap around your wrist once plaited.

5 Plait three ribbons together.

6 As you plait, thread in the charms at regular intervals. Tie off the end, then your creations are ready to wear!

TRY THIS!

Some types of shrink plastic can be printed on. Check that you have the right type, though.

Rapunzel

Thin cord or beads could be plaited into your bracelet.

Ariel

Fork, which Ariel names a "dinglehopper".

Cinderella

Tiana

Snow White

Choose coloured ribbons to represent each princess.

Memory Spheres

In Riley's mind, her memories are stored in balls called memory spheres. Record your own memories in these spheres that double up as colourful decorations. Each one is unique to you!

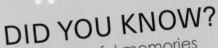

DID YOU KNOW?
Riley's joyful memories are yellow orbs. Her sad memories are blue, disgusting ones are green, angry ones are red and frightening ones are purple.

You will need:

- Clear plastic spheres that divide in half
- PVA glue
- Sponge or tissues
- Gold glitter
- Newspaper or protective cover
- Objects that remind you of happy times
- Gold bows or ribbon
- Gold thread

Frame your memories
Many craft shops sell clear plastic spheres that divide in half. They make great display cases for special objects or pictures.

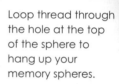

Spread the glue right up to the edges.

1 Separate a sphere into its two halves.

2 Coat the inside of one half with PVA glue.

3 Use a sponge or tissue to spread the glue evenly. Cover the whole surface.

4 Dust the inside with gold glitter. Shake the excess out onto newspaper. Then carefully tip it back into the container. Leave the inside to dry.

5 Put a special object that reminds you of a happy memory inside the half-sphere. Make sure it's facing outwards. You could glue it in place.

6 Put the two halves of the sphere together.

7 Glue a gold bow to the top or tie one with gold ribbon.

Loop thread through the hole at the top of the sphere to hang up your memory spheres.

Spheres can be opened up and put back together again and again.

Gold glitter represents happy memories.

Only you know what the objects inside mean to you!

TOP TIP
As well as objects, you could put photographs of happy memories in your spheres.

Hairclip Organiser

Use the power of Rapunzel's hair to organise your hair accessories. This beautiful plait will stop your hairclips from getting tangled or lost – and it displays them beautifully, too.

You will need:

- Measuring tape
- Scissors
- 12 strands of yellow wool, 80 cm (32 in) long
- 80 strands of yellow wool, 160 cm (63 in) long
- Extra yellow wool
- 80 cm (32 in) of narrow, pink ribbon
- 80 cm (32 in) of narrow, purple ribbon
- Wide, purple ribbon (enough for two bows)

Mini plait

Cut the wool and ribbons before you start. This plait will be woven into the main plait.

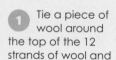

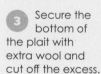

1 Tie a piece of wool around the top of the 12 strands of wool and cut off the excess.

2 Divide the strands into three sections. Plait together.

3 Secure the bottom of the plait with extra wool and cut off the excess.

Plait it all together

All the strands of wool are folded in half. This makes the plait chunkier and also gives a neat finish to its top.

1 Gather together the long pieces of wool and fold them in half.

2 Place the mini plait and the two thin pieces of ribbon on top of the wool.

3 Tie a short piece of wool around the whole bunch, just below the fold.

4 Divide the wool into three equal sections: one with the thin plait another with the pink ribbon and the other with the purple ribbon.

TOP TIP

To create a neat, tight plait , ask someone to hold the end of the plait or fasten it to something that won't move.

Ribbon bows hide the wool that secures the plait

Hairgrips easily clip on and off the woollen hair.

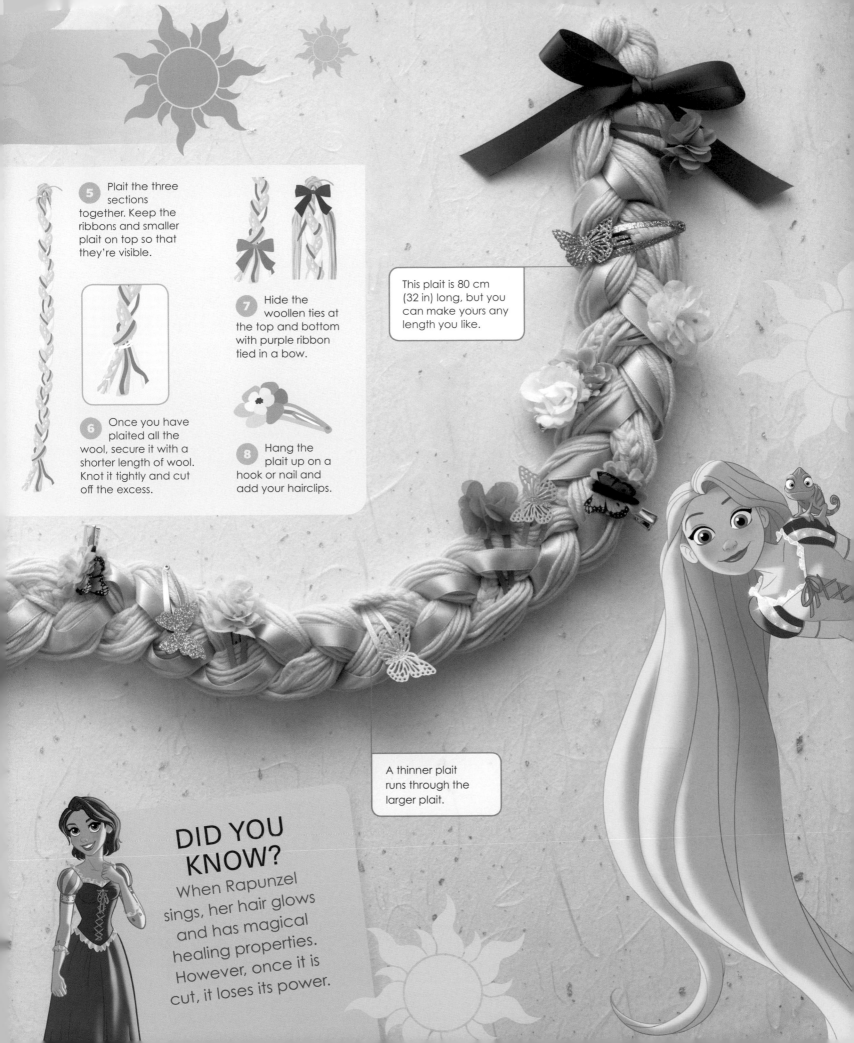

5 Plait the three sections together. Keep the ribbons and smaller plait on top so that they're visible.

7 Hide the woollen ties at the top and bottom with purple ribbon tied in a bow.

6 Once you have plaited all the wool, secure it with a shorter length of wool. Knot it tightly and cut off the excess.

8 Hang the plait up on a hook or nail and add your hairclips.

This plait is 80 cm (32 in) long, but you can make yours any length you like.

A thinner plait runs through the larger plait.

DID YOU KNOW?
When Rapunzel sings, her hair glows and has magical healing properties. However, once it is cut, it loses its power.

Friendship Necklaces

Do you have a friend who loves Disney? Share a token of friendship with them with this necklace that becomes two keepsakes. Treasure one half yourself and give the other to someone special.

You will need:

- Paper
- Pencil
- Scissors
- Polymer clay
- Rolling pin
- Cling film
- Table knife
- Oven
- Baking tray
- Drinking straw
- PVA glue
- Coloured cord or ribbon

Make a template

Mickey Mouse's head is an iconic but simple shape. Draw three overlapping circles to make it. You could draw around circular objects such as coins or lids.

1 Draw Mickey's head on a piece of paper. Cut it out to create your template.

Roll your clay

You could roll out a single colour of clay, but for a more original, unique necklace, marble together different colours.

1 Pre-heat the oven, following the clay package instructions.

2 Choose colours that you think will blend together well.

3 To marble, start with a ball of one colour 2.5 cm (1 in) in diameter and add mini balls of other colours on top.

4 Roll it all out, adding more tiny balls until you like the pattern.

5 Keep going until you get a nice mix of colours and the clay is roughly 0.5 cm (⅕ in) thick.

Make the necklace

Now that you have your template and your clay, you can shape and bake your necklace.

1 Place your Mickey template on the clay and carefully cut around it with a table knife.

2 Make a hole in each ear with the drinking straw.

3 Cut a zig-zag line through the middle of the shape to divide it into two pendants.

4 Place both parts on a baking tray.

To get a striped pattern, use sausage shapes of different colours rolled together.

Sparkly details created by adding scraps of foil to the clay.

5 Ask an adult to bake it in the oven, following the package instructions. Leave to cool.

6 Varnish the pendant with a coat of PVA glue. This makes it nice and shiny.

7 To turn your pendant into a necklace, fold your chosen cord or ribbon in half. Thread it through your pre-made hole.

8 Thread the ends through the loop and pull it tight. Tie the ends loosely so that you can easily take it on and off.

TOP TIP
When you roll the clay, place cling film over the top to keep the clay clean.

Recycled Robot

WALL·E is a robot designed to clean up waste by crushing it into cubes. Why not recycle some of your rubbish by using it to build your own WALL·E? He's the perfect junk-modelling project.

You will need:

- Cardboard tubes
- Corrugated cardboard
- Scissors
- Glue
- 2 plastic pods from a coffee machine
- 150 ml (5fl oz) fizzy drink can
- Square cardboard box
- Brown paper or paint
- Acrylic paint
- Paintbrush
- Thin cardboard
- 2 metallic bendy straws
- Pencil
- Double-sided tape (optional)

Make WALL·E's wheels

WALL·E can cover all sorts of uneven terrain thanks to the treads on his wheels.

Tubes with different diameters make the wheels look more like WALL·E's.

1 Trim six tubes so they are all the same length.

2 Glue the tubes together, in two groups of three.

3 Cut two strips of corrugated cardboard, long and wide enough to wrap around each group of tubes.

If the corrugated cardboard has two outer layers, peel off one side to expose the ridges.

4 Wrap each strip around a group of tubes and glue in place.

Make WALL·E's eyes

Make cardboard and coffee pods look like camera lenses, resembling WALL·E's audio-visual sensors.

1 Tape the end of each coffee pod onto the end of a cardboard tube.

2 Cut two strips of corrugated cardboard and wrap a piece around each pod to make a teardrop shape.

3 Glue the eyes together so the teardrop shapes curve together.

Bring it all together

The waste-compacting section of WALL·E's body forms the central part of this recycled robot.

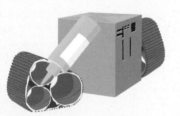

1 Paint the box brown or wrap it in brown paper. Add on WALL·E's markings in black paint.

2 Stick the wheels on the body using glue or double-sided tape.

3 Cut out two small, thin cardboard squares for hands. Cut out a small section from each.

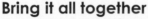

Secure with glue if needed.

4 Cut a small slit in the long end of each straw, then slot in a hand piece.

5 Ask an adult to use a pencil to pierce two holes in the box, one above each wheel. Insert a straw in each side.

Bendy straws allow WALL·E's arms to move.

6 Paint the fizzy drink can gold.

7 Attach the eyes to the can with glue or double-sided tape. Glue or tape this onto the top of the box.

DID YOU KNOW?
WALL•E stands for "Waste Allocation Load Lifter: Earth Class". He befriends an "Extraterrestrial Vegetation Evaluator", or EVE for short.

Instead of a can, you could use a painted cardboard tube for the neck.

Most packaging boxes are corrugated cardboard, but have two outer layers.

Egg-Box Bugs

Flik is an inventive ant, always coming up with new ways of looking at things. Here's a creative way of making him and his friends. You could build a whole colony of these colourful characters from egg boxes!

You will need:

- Six-count egg box
- Scissors
- Paint
- Paintbrush
- Pencil
- 6–8 pipe cleaners for each ant
- Glue
- Sticky tape
- Black pen

Cut your box

These egg-box pieces can be used to make Flik or any other ant character from the colony.

1 Cut the lid off the egg box.

2 Cut the box down the middle so that you have two rows of three cups.

3 Neaten the shape with scissors.

4 Cut row B so that it is shallower than row A. Row B should then fit inside row A.

5 Cut the bottom cups of both rows in half, so the rows stand up easily.

Cut along here.

Bring it all together

Now's the time for your eggs to hatch into bugs!

You might need adult help when making these holes.

1 Paint both egg-box rows blue.

2 With a pencil, make two holes at the bottom of row A for legs.

3 Push a blue pipe cleaner in each leg hole.

4 Bend each leg to make a knee. Curl both ends to make feet.

5 Secure the pipe cleaners on the inside of the box with sticky tape.

6 With a pencil, make two tiny holes in the top of row B for the antennae.

7 Attach two blue pipe cleaners for antennae.

8 Bend each antenna in the middle and then curl at the end.

9 Make two more holes in the sides of row B for arms.

10 Add two pipe-cleaner arms. Bend them in the middle and curl them at the ends to make hands.

Egg-box shape looks like a nose

Bend pipe cleaners to change the poses and expressions.

11 Glue row B inside row A and leave to dry.

12 Paint on large white eyes and a mouth.

13 Once dry, add detail to the eyes with black pen.

Pose your characters by bending their pipe-cleaner limbs.

Flik

Princess Atta

TOP TIP
If you have any holes in the box, cover them with masking tape before you paint.

DID YOU KNOW?
Princess Atta is the crown princess ant. She's learning how to rule the colony so that she can take over from her ageing mother, the Queen.

Atta alternative
With a few tweaks to the method used to make Flik, you can craft Atta, too.

1. Paint your egg boxes purple.

2. After you've added arms, legs and antennae, make two more holes in row B for wings.

3. For each wing, bend a purple pipe cleaner into a loop, twisting the ends into a single point.

4. Push the point of each wing through a hole and secure on the inside with tape.

5. Stick the boxes together.

6. Cut green paper to make Atta's crown, and glue it onto her head.

7. Add eyelashes with black pen.

B   A

Olaf Sock Toy

Do you want to build a snowman? You don't need to wait for snow with this all-weather Olaf. He can even be made in summer. Follow these steps to make the happiest snowman around!

Get prepared

Olaf is a very unique snowman. Use felt to capture his cool features – like his big smile and twig hair!

1. Cut out pieces of coloured felt.

Two eyebrows

Tooth

Orange semicircle nose   *Hair*   *Three buttons*   *Two arms*   *Mouth*

You will need:

- Felt (black and orange)
- Scissors
- White sock
- Small, clear elastic bands
- Uncooked rice
- PVA glue
- Googly eyes
- Two white pom-poms

Transform your sock

Filled with rice, your Olaf will be sturdy enough to stand up easily by himself.

1. Measure 200 g (7 oz) of rice and pour it into the bottom of the sock.

2. Push the rice down so it's tightly packed and forms a ball.

3. Secure the sock above the ball of rice with an elastic band.

Trim the top of the sock if it's too tall.

Measure 150 g (5¼ oz) of rice for the head.

Measure 100 g (3½ oz) of rice for the stomach.

4. Repeat steps 1 to 3 to fill his body. Take note of the different quantities of rice.

5. Use glue to secure the balls to each other.

6. Roll up the orange felt to make a cone like a carrot, and glue it together.

7. Glue the carrot nose and eyes onto the face.

8. Glue on the black and brown felt.

9. Glue the white tooth on top of Olaf's mouth.

10. Glue two pom-pom feet to the body. Be careful not to glue everything to the table.

DID YOU KNOW?

Olaf was created by Elsa's magic. This walking, talking, dancing snowman is always willing to lend a stick hand to those in need.

Use clear elastic bands because the top one will be visible.

Snowgies appear when Elsa sneezes.

Snowgies

Olaf

Snowgie friends
Give Olaf some company with these adorable mini Snowgies. All you need are white pom-poms, black felt and glue.

1 Cut out small mouths and eyes from black felt.

2 Glue together two white pom-poms.

3 Add two tiny pom-pom feet.

4 Glue on the felt face details.

Templates

These templates will help you make many of the projects in this book. For best results, lay tracing paper onto the template and trace over its outline with a sharp pencil. Then turn the tracing paper over and place it on the material you wish to cut out. Trace over the shape on the back of the tracing paper with the pencil. When you lift the paper up, you will see the pencil marks have been transferred to your material. Now you can cut out the shape, or colour it in.

Flamingo Croquet
page 53

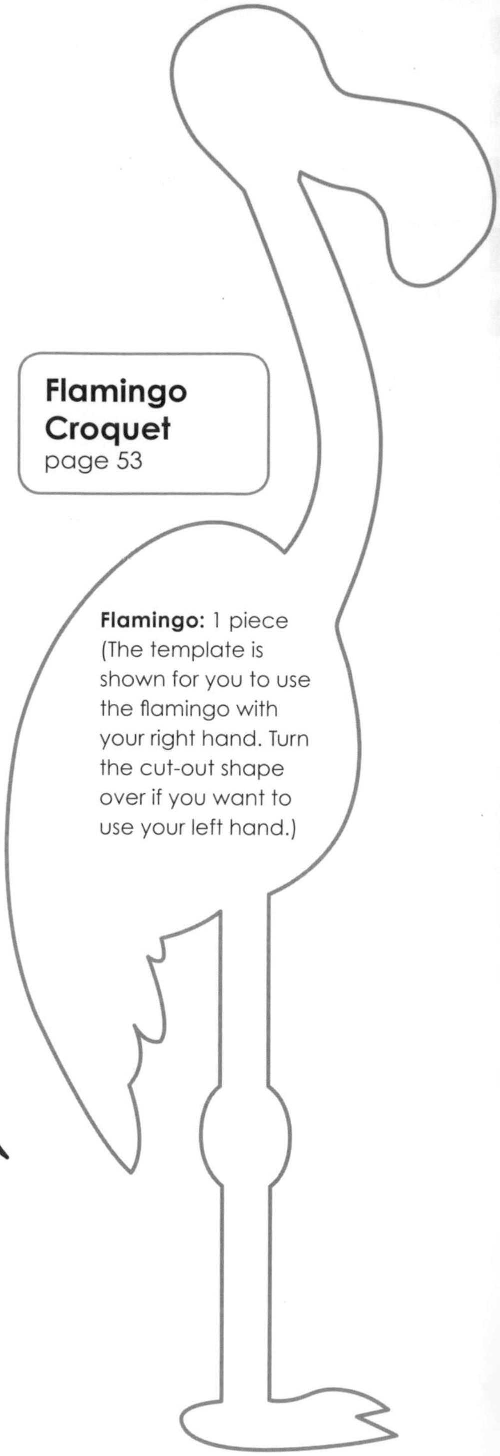

Flamingo: 1 piece (The template is shown for you to use the flamingo with your right hand. Turn the cut-out shape over if you want to use your left hand.)

Felt Animal Masks
pages 18–19

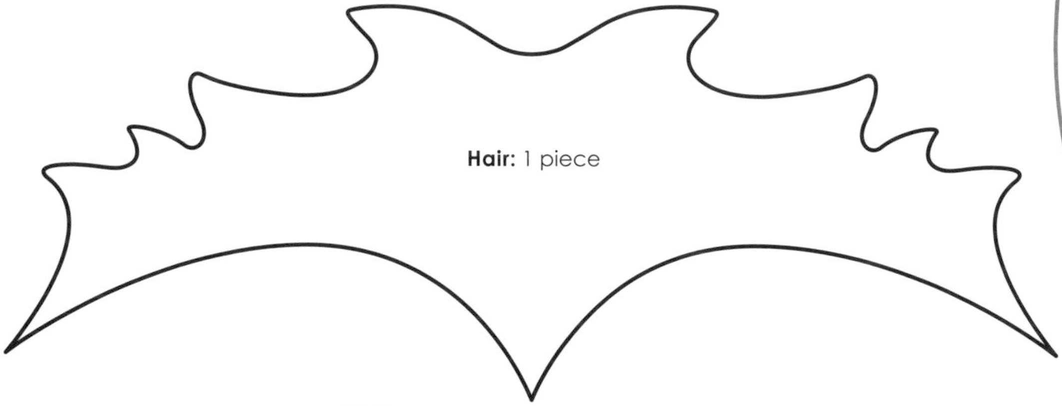

Hair: 1 piece

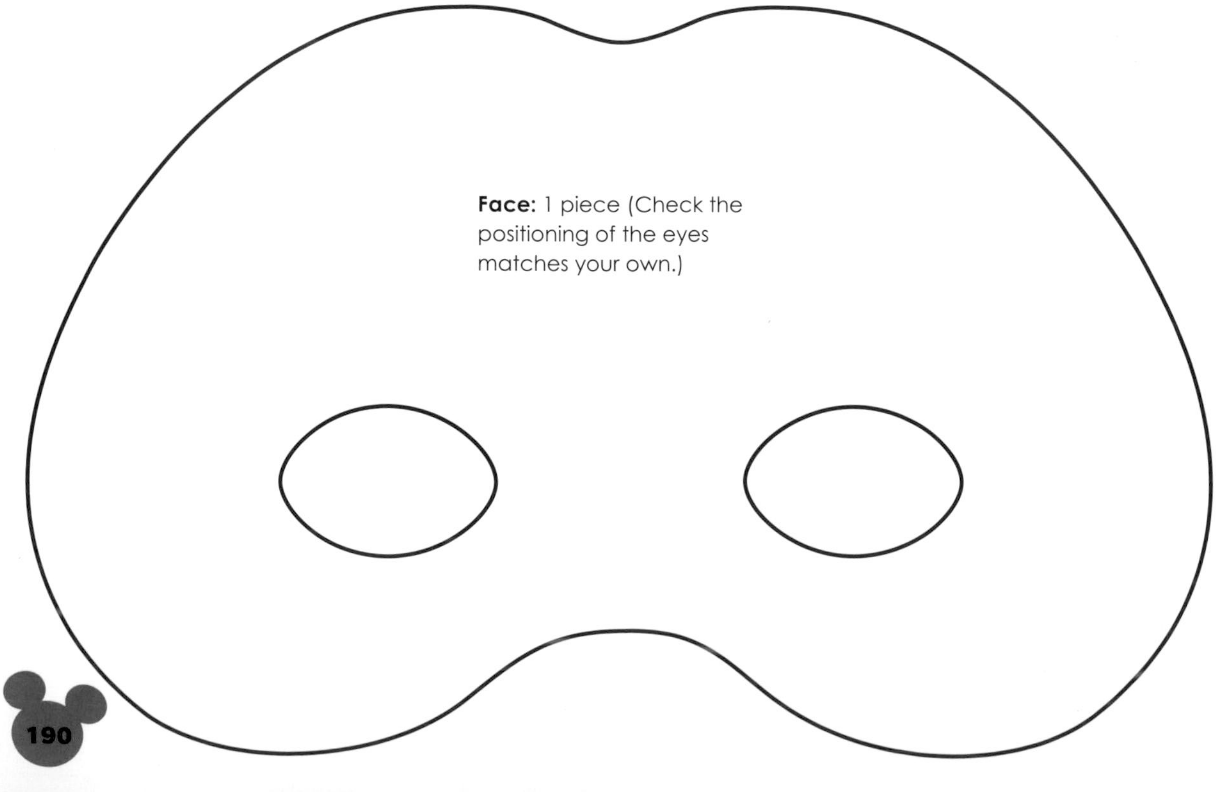

Face: 1 piece (Check the positioning of the eyes matches your own.)

Ear: 2 pieces

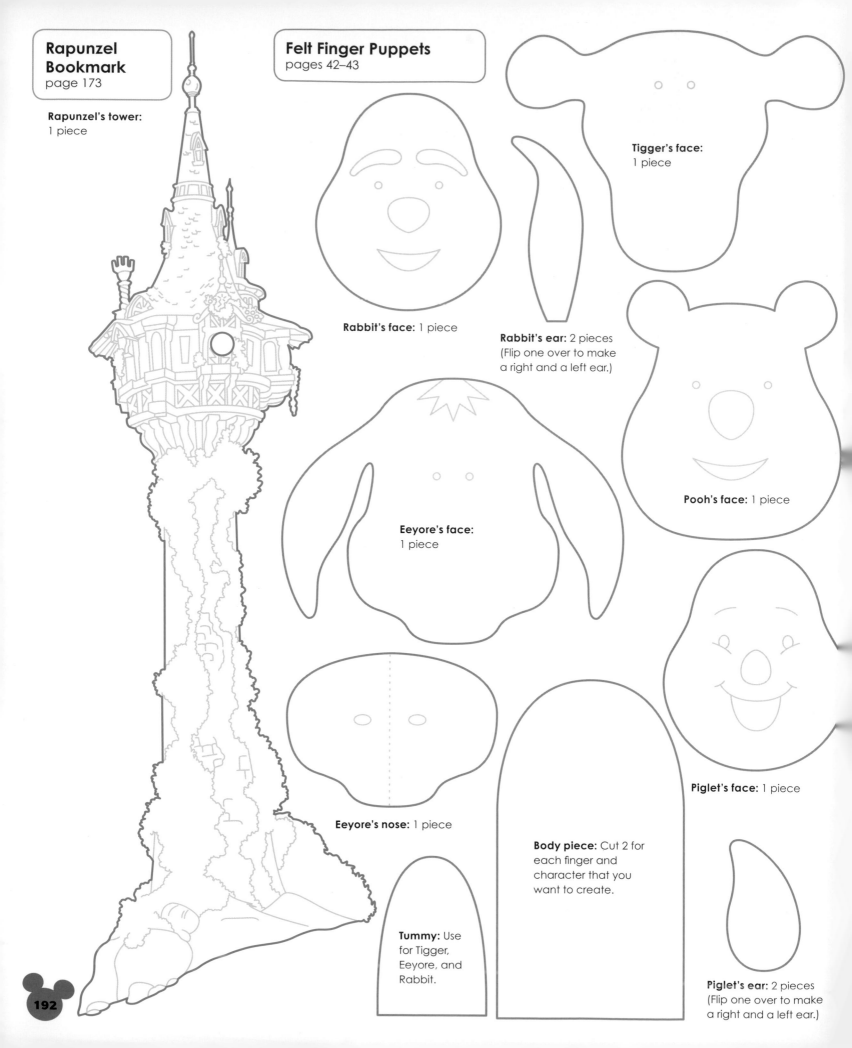

Rapunzel Bookmark
page 173

Rapunzel's tower:
1 piece

Felt Finger Puppets
pages 42–43

Rabbit's face: 1 piece

Tigger's face:
1 piece

Rabbit's ear: 2 pieces
(Flip one over to make
a right and a left ear.)

Eyore's face:
1 piece

Pooh's face: 1 piece

Eyore's nose: 1 piece

Body piece: Cut 2 for
each finger and
character that you
want to create.

Piglet's face: 1 piece

Tummy: Use
for Tigger,
Eyore, and
Rabbit.

Piglet's ear: 2 pieces
(Flip one over to make
a right and a left ear.)

Tigger's ear:
2 pieces (Flip one over to make a right and a left ear.)

Tigger's nose:
1 piece

Tigger's mouth:
1 piece

Balloon Faces
pages 102–103

Dawn Bellwether's eyebrow:
2 pieces (Flip one over to make a right and a left eyebrow.)

Dawn Bellwether's eye:
2 pieces (Flip one over to make a right and a left eye.)

Dawn Bellwether's hair: 1 piece

Dawn Bellwether's nose and mouth: 1 piece

Dawn Bellwether's ear:
2 pieces (Flip one over to make a right and a left ear.)

Dawn Bellwether's glasses: 1 piece

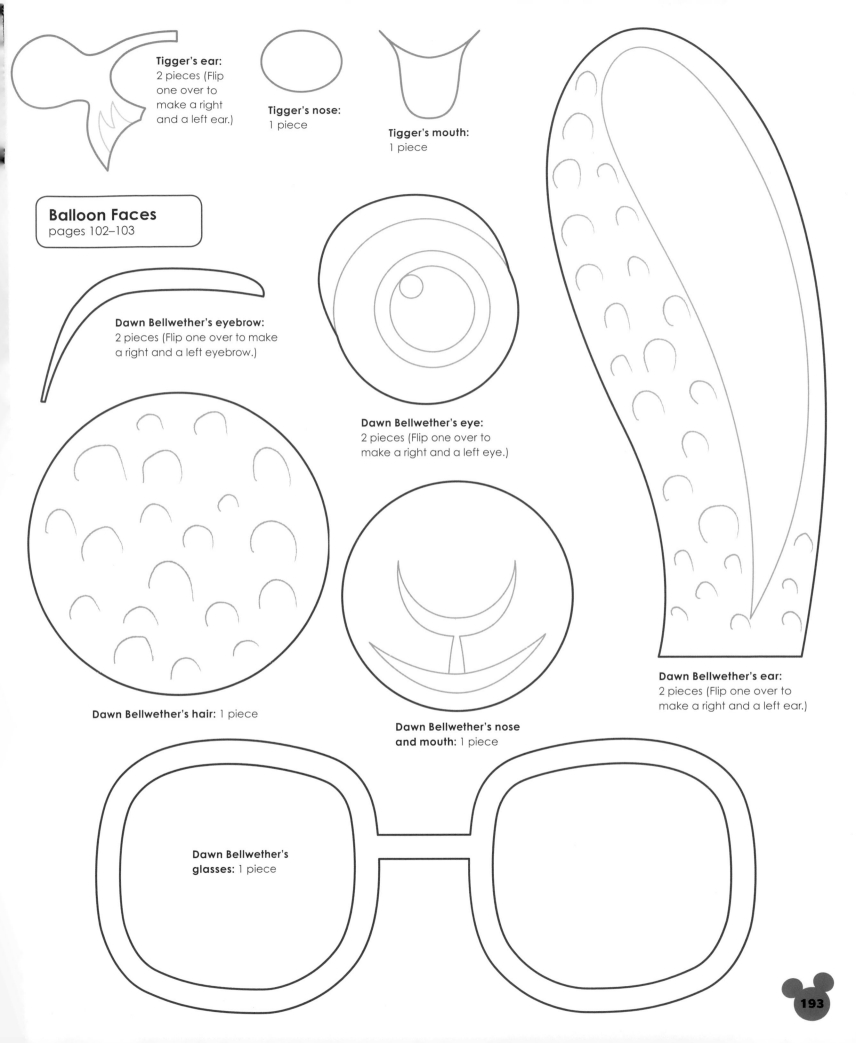

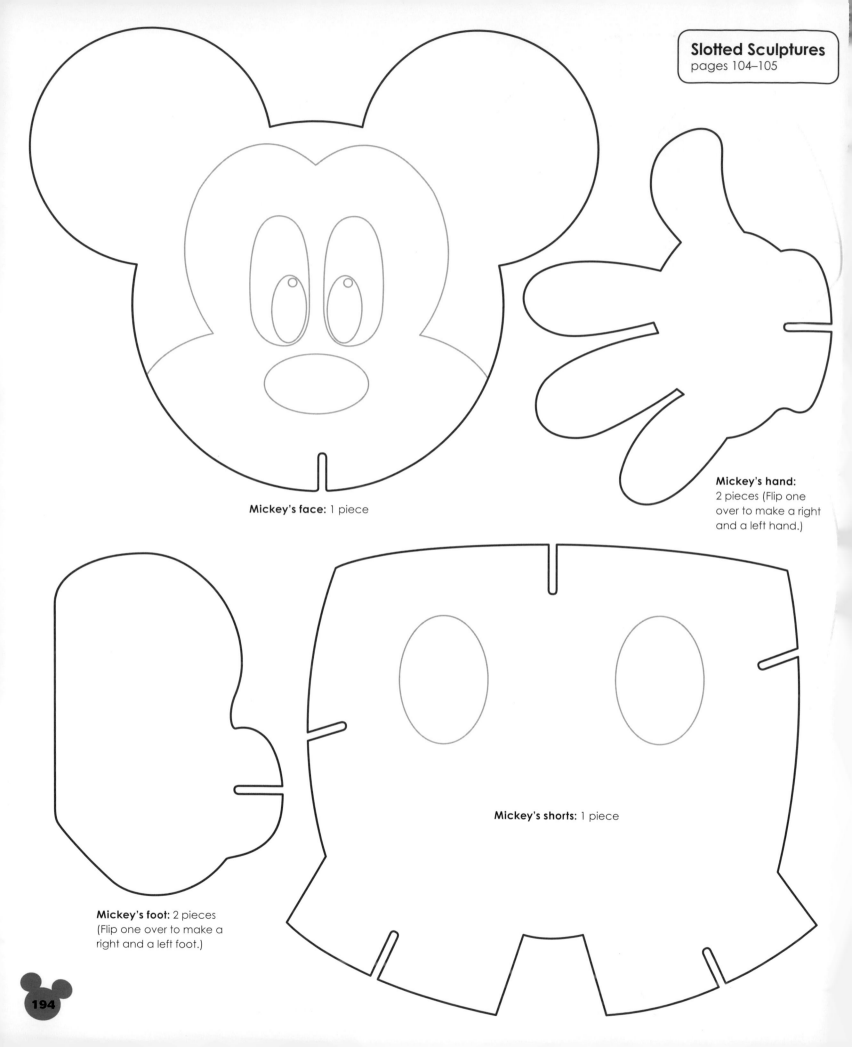

Mickey's face: 1 piece

Mickey's hand: 2 pieces (Flip one over to make a right and a left hand.)

Mickey's foot: 2 pieces (Flip one over to make a right and a left foot.)

Mickey's shorts: 1 piece

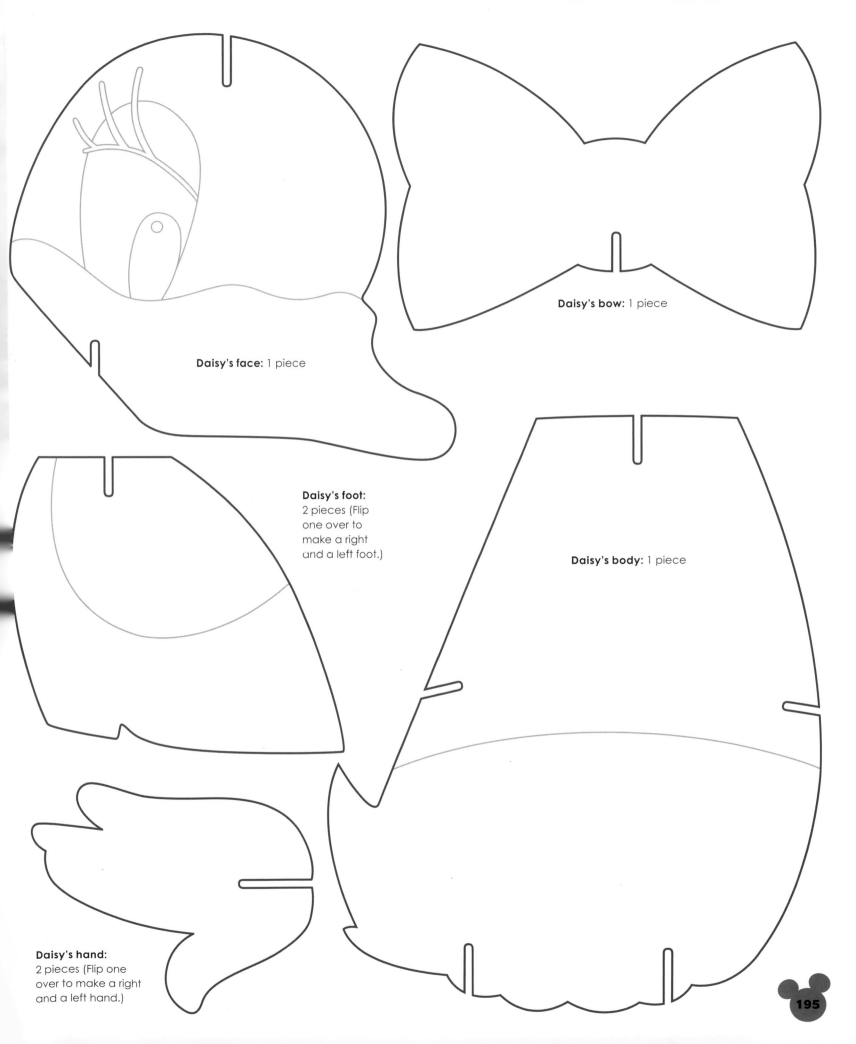

Daisy's face: 1 piece

Daisy's bow: 1 piece

Daisy's foot:
2 pieces (Flip
one over to
make a right
and a left foot.)

Daisy's body: 1 piece

Daisy's hand:
2 pieces (Flip one
over to make a right
and a left hand.)

195

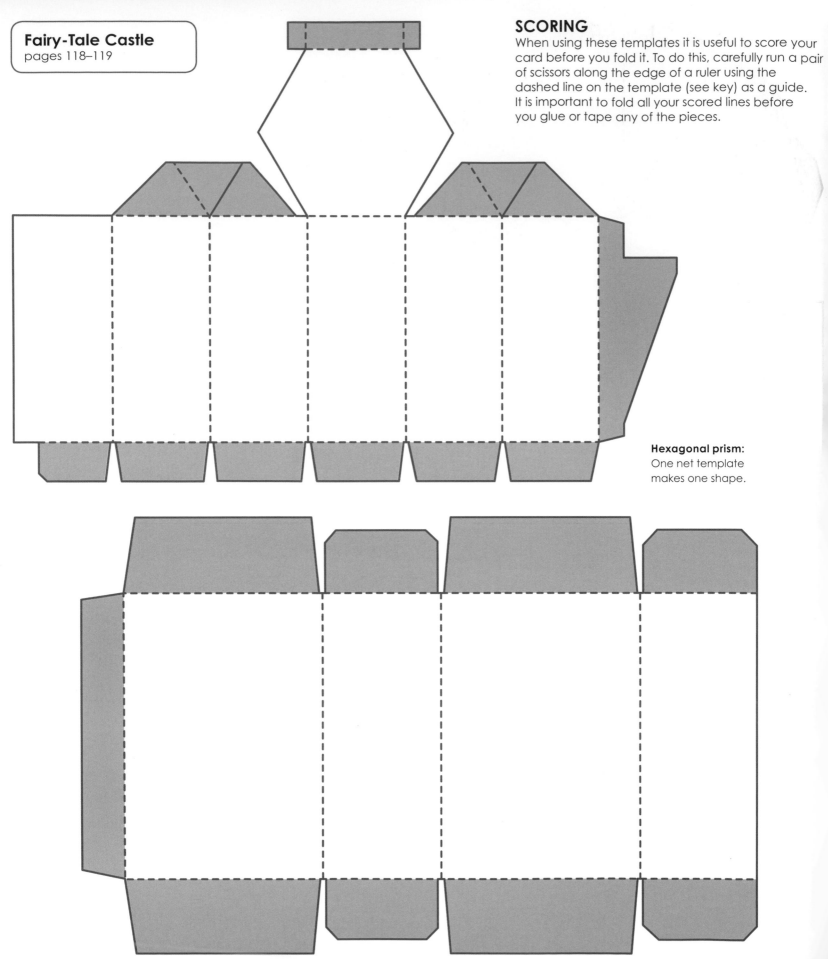

SCORING

When using these templates it is useful to score your card before you fold it. To do this, carefully run a pair of scissors along the edge of a ruler using the dashed line on the template (see key) as a guide. It is important to fold all your scored lines before you glue or tape any of the pieces.

Hexagonal prism:
One net template makes one shape.

Cuboids: One net template makes one shape.

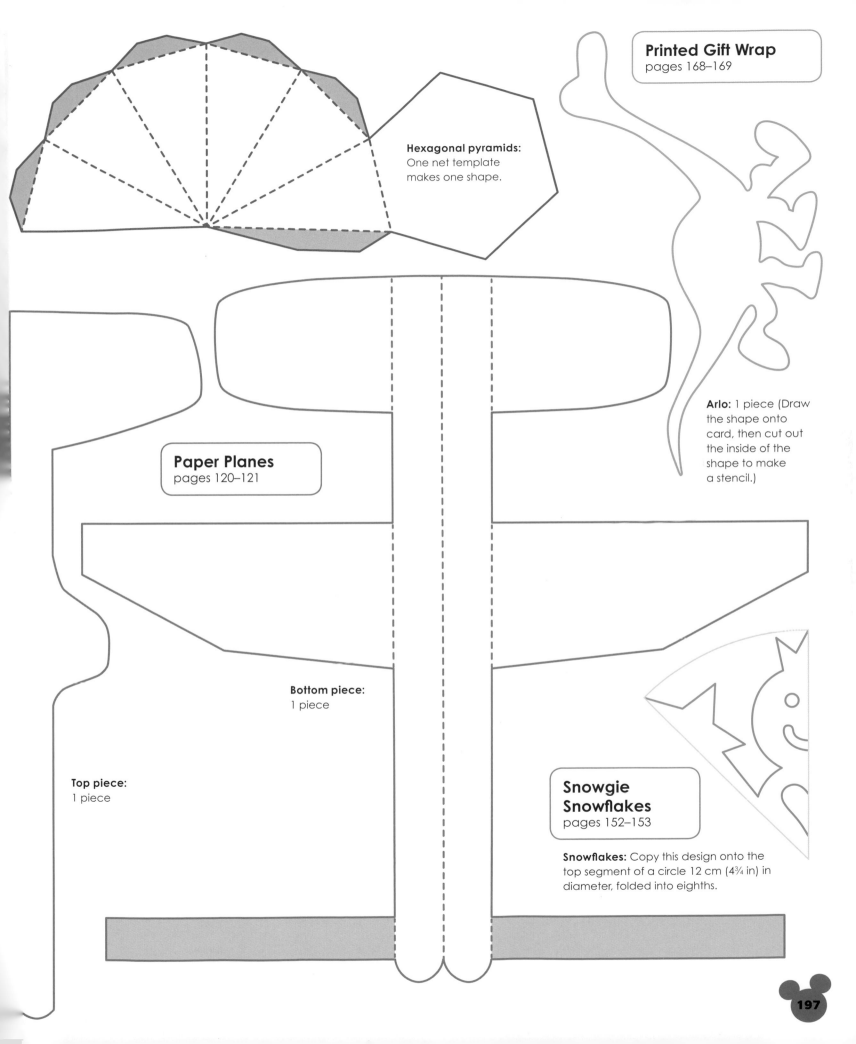

Hexagonal pyramids:
One net template
makes one shape.

Printed Gift Wrap
pages 168–169

Arlo: 1 piece (Draw
the shape onto
card, then cut out
the inside of the
shape to make
a stencil.)

Paper Planes
pages 120–121

Bottom piece:
1 piece

Top piece:
1 piece

**Snowgie
Snowflakes**
pages 152–153

Snowflakes: Copy this design onto the
top segment of a circle 12 cm (4¾ in) in
diameter, folded into eighths.

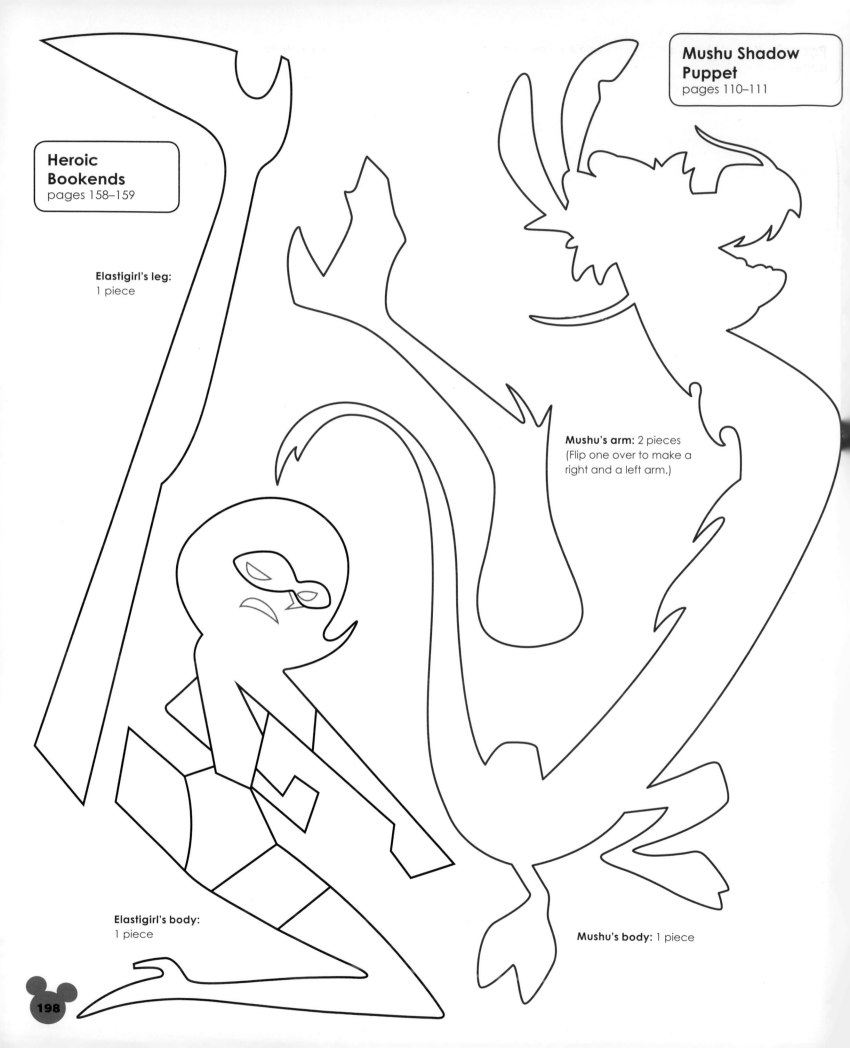

Mushu Shadow Puppet
pages 110–111

Heroic Bookends
pages 158–159

Elastigirl's leg:
1 piece

Mushu's arm: 2 pieces
(Flip one over to make a
right and a left arm.)

Elastigirl's body:
1 piece

Mushu's body: 1 piece

198

Parachuting Soldiers
pages 66–67

Soldiers: Cut 2 of each (Flip one over to make the front and the back of your soldier.)

Party Hats
pages 164–165

Pooh's ear: 2 pieces (Cut out separately; flip one over to make a right and a left ear.)

Hat cone: 1 piece (Cut or colour facial features separately.)

T-shirt: 1 piece (Cut or colour separately.)

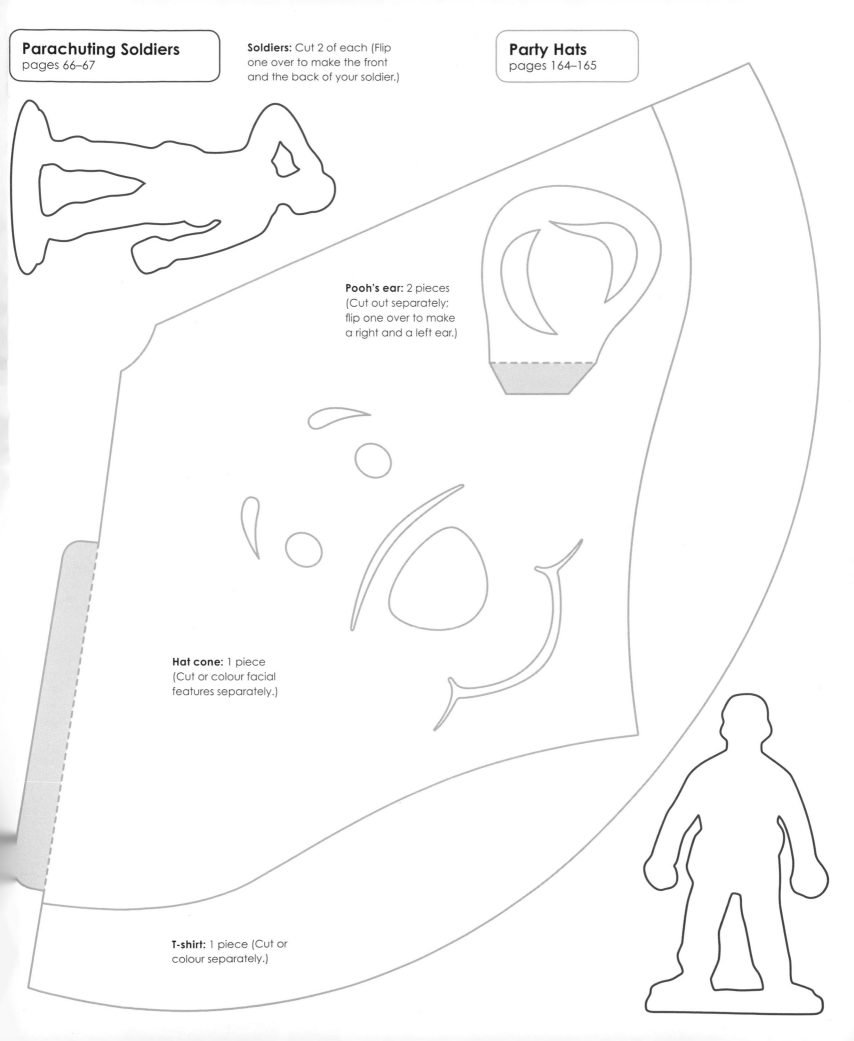

Senior Editors Emma Grange, Elizabeth Dowsett
Senior Designers Lynne Moulding, Joe Scott
Project Editor Lisa Stock
Project Art Editor Jenny Edwards
Designers Rosamund Bird, Lisa Sodeau
Editorial Assistant Natalie Edwards
Design Assistant Akiko Kato
Pre-production Producer Siu Yin Chan
Senior Producer Mary Slater
Managing Editor Sadie Smith
Managing Art Editor Vicky Short
DTP Designers Sunil Sharma, Radjeep Singh
Publisher Julie Ferris
Art Director Lisa Lanzarini Öhlander
Publishing Director Simon Beecroft

Illustrations by Lynne Moulding
Model Creators Dominique Sayers, Little Button Diaries,
Akiko Kato, Lynne Moulding, Natalie Edwards, Anni Sander,
Jade Wheaton, Vicky Short, Lisa Lanzarini and Emma Grange
Photography by Dave King and Lol Johnson

First published in Great Britain in 2018 by
Dorling Kindersley Limited
80 Strand, London, WC2R 0RL
A Penguin Random House Company

18 19 20 21 22 10 9 8 7 6 5 4 3 2 1
001–307680–Oct/2018

Acknowledgements

DK would like to thank: Disney Family for inspiration,
and the permission to reproduce some of their
wonderful projects; Chelsea Alon, Julia Vargas,
and Stephanie Everett at Disney Publishing; Gary
Ombler and Clare Winfield for extra photography work;
Charlie Goodge for photography assistance; Dena
and Tali Stock for concept generation; Nicola Torode
and MTS for safety consultancy; Eitan and Joshua
Black, Florence Hatswell, Lady Arianna Nyamteh,
Lily Maia Öhlander, Amari and Nevaeh Osivwemu,
and Alex Park for modelling; Tim Quince for picture
research; Chris Gould, Rhys Thomas, and Abi Wright
for design assistance; Shari Last and Matt Jones
for additional editorial work; US editors Kayla Dugger
and Lori Hand; Julia March for proofreading and
anglicising; Jane Bull for expert crafting assistance;
and Elizabeth Dowsett for writing.

The author would like to thank: all the editors and
designers at DK, particularly Lisa Stock and Lynne
Moulding. Thanks to Emma Grange, Natalie Edwards
and the crafters who have brought all the ideas to life
so brilliantly. Thank you also to Vivienne Pinnington and
Lisa Parkes for inspiration about how to recreate the
world of Disney at home. Finally, thank you to Emily and
Toby – two big Disney fans and prolific crafters.